BURDENS to Blessings

Kim Crabill

D1512036

BroadStreet
PUBLISHING

BroadStreet Publishing Group, LLC
Racine, Wisconsin, USA
BroadStreetPublishing.com

BURDENS *To Blessings: Discover the Power of Your Story*

Stock or custom editions of BroadStreet Publishing titles may be purchased in bulk for educational, business, ministry, fundraising, or sales promotional use. For information, please e-mail info@broadstreetpublishing.com.

Cover design by Chris Garborg, garborgdesign.com
Interior design and typeset by Katherine Lloyd, TheDESKonline.com

Printed in the United States of America

16 17 18 19 20 5 4 3 2 1

To my mother,
whose final choice of honesty
freed me to live in truth.

TABLE OF CONTENTS

Brown-Bag Burdens

*(What You Need to Know
Before You Read Any Further)*

I t all began in our local grocery store. I had prepared for the Bible study I'd be leading the next day and was now grabbing a few snacks for our introductory session. As I walked down the paper goods aisle, I had this overwhelming urge to purchase, of all things, brown paper lunch bags. Now, I have to stop here and explain why this urge was so phenomenal. You see, as a Southern-born-and-bred woman, I don't "do" ugly brown bags! I prefer raspberry and lime green with a hint of polka dots or powder-pink with an orange sherbet stripe. A brown paper bag would never enter my mind except as an object of derision. So you can imagine my dilemma as I stood looking at those bags and thinking that the urge to purchase them was a "divine" urge. I was pretty sure I was not only supposed to buy them, but also to hand them out to my guests.

Oh no, no, NO! I plowed on past the bags, determined to ignore my urge. *You'll be sorry!* was the next thought to enter my mind. *Do you really want to fight these crowds again just to come back and buy those ugly bags? Because you* will *be buying them!*

Who is talking? I asked myself (though I was pretty sure I knew). *Is this a joke?* (Again, I knew the answer to my own question—it wasn't a joke.) I reversed my cart and returned to the aisle with the paper bags. Just looking at them made me cringe.

I tried bargaining. *You know,* I suggested, *if—and I mean if—I really will need paper bags I will just stroll on over to the gift wrapping section. At least there I can buy some pretty bags! I can coordinate with the season or, even better, with my kitchen décor!*

I was pretty proud of my proposed compromise, but the insistent voice was not. *No! Not raspberry and lime green with a hint of polka dots, not powder pink with an orange sherbet stripe, not seasonal, not even trendy taupe . . . only plain old brown paper bags will do.*

We all have "brown paper bags" that we carry around to hold our hurts.

With my confusion and frustration rising, I grabbed the silly bags and stuck them in the back of the grocery cart underneath the raspberry-colored toilet paper.

Driving home, doubts crept in. "God, was that You? As crazy as this sounds, are You behind this brown bag incident in which I just embarrassed myself at the grocery store?"

Turns out He *was* behind it, and soon I knew why.

Ladies, Pack Your Bags

Standing before the group the next morning, I gave each woman in the room an ugly brown paper bag. Then I asked, "If you could pack anything in this bag that you would like to eat, what would it be?" What a wonderful icebreaker! Our answers told a lot about who we were and where we came from. It was fun! But no one was prepared for my next question: "What's in the bag that's eating at you?"

Over the course of the previous evening, I had again asked God, "Why the bags?" Then I spent time listening for His answer. I began to realize we all have "brown paper bags" that we carry around to hold our hurts, tragedies, disappointments, unfulfilled dreams, abuses, addictions, and more. None of us, Southern or not, like these bags. We just aren't quite sure what to do with them. We try to hide them. And, oh yes, we definitely try to pretty them up with our busy little lives, happy little smiles, and peppy little personalities. But no matter what we do, we know they are there, don't we? I can say this so assuredly because I carried around my bag for more than twenty-five years.

The worse part about bags and their burdensome contents is that they eat away at us no matter how cleverly we try to deny their existence. They nibble at our peace and happiness. They erode our confidence and competence. They gobble up our sense of self-worth. Then, when opportunities come—to serve in our churches, to be a PTA officer, to invite a new neighbor for coffee, to just participate in life—our damaged selves respond in one of two ways: We say yes to all of it to prove our bags cannot hold us hostage, or we decline every opportunity out of fear that participation of any sort will expose what's in our bags. Either way, our bags full of burdens rob us of real life.

I knew God was behind the brown bag idea because He and I had previously "done business" with my own brown bag. As I found the courage to open my bag and let God see what was in it, I found an amazing thing: God was standing there in the ugly brown bag! He wasn't put off by my hurts and burdens; He was right in the midst of them, and *He was waiting for me there!*

That's a long story that will unfold as you read this book. For now, get yourself an ugly brown paper bag. Don't feel pressured to do anything with it yet. Eventually, chapter by chapter, you'll discover ways to use your bag. At times, you'll want to stash things in the bag. At other times, you'll feel led to take a fresh look at its contents. The bag will become something unique for each woman who uses this book, but one thing will remain the same for everyone: When you look in your bag, *God will be there.*

And because of His presence, all those things that have been eating at you will get transformed. From within that ugly bag of burdens will spill forth blessings that God will use to refresh and feed you and the multitude of hurting people all around you. So grab your brown bag and let's get started.

CHAPTER ONE

A Princess Story Goes Wrong

I have found that when a person finds the courage to be herself and share her story, it gives those around her the freedom to be similarly vulnerable and transparent. This is where burdens become blessings. With that outcome in mind, I begin my story.

Travel with me back to 1962. I was four years old and living in a small town tucked near the Blue Ridge Parkway with a mom, a dad, two brothers, and two sisters. Being the youngest, I was the princess. Not that I was surrounded by royal trumpeters or ladies-in-waiting, but I was surrounded by my daddy's love. Every time he looked at me, his big smile let me know how much he loved me.

I couldn't imagine anything better than life in this small town. I delighted in waking each morning to the sound of WBOB, the local radio station, and the smell of bacon on the stove. Even my regular chores were made fun by the fact that, after they were done, I could spend time in my palace—an old reconstructed coal shed. Every afternoon at 3:00, with Mama close behind, I would run down the steps of our white-framed house, across the train tracks, and into the heart of our town where I would watch for Daddy's head to pop up over the hill as he made his way home from the textile mill. He always made me giggle at his look of surprise that I was there. Even though he was exhausted from a long day of shift work, he would break into his big smile. That was my signal to start running—right into the arms of this man who loved me so much. I can recall the sense of security I would feel each time I tucked my hand in his to begin our walk home. My dad was six foot four, so my arm would soon become completely numb from holding it up so high for so long to maintain my grasp of his hand. But that was OK—I sure wasn't letting go!

The Day I'll Never Forget

The day I'll never forget began as a beautiful autumn day in Virginia. The leaves glistened with changing colors. The air was crisp and cool. As I headed to my palace to play, I had no reason to expect that this wouldn't be another great day for a four-year-old princess.

When I heard Mama and Daddy calling me to come in, I wasn't surprised. I had noticed company arriving. But when I walked through the front door I was startled by the mood in our little home. It seemed so gloomy. And why were all eyes on me? I lowered my head, hiding behind my long blonde curls. I felt embarrassed.

Mama was holding my "church dress," my black patent leather shoes, and my favorite hair bows. Even though I noticed the sad look on her face, I felt a rush of excitement as she told me I was going to wear my favorite clothes to a very special place that day. But then I saw something I had never seen before: tears sliding down Mama's face.

Later that evening, dressed in my Sunday best, I stood at the back of the church, waiting, with a rice packet in one hand and my packed suitcase in the other. I kept replaying Mama's strange words to me: "Kim, you know how much we love you. You must always remember that. But today, things will change. You are not going to live with us anymore. Kim, I know this will be very hard but promise me that you will try to be a big girl."

As the organ's music neared its end, I began to understand that life as I had always known it was ending as well.

It would take years for me to understand that Mama and Daddy were not my biological parents. They were my grandparents. Linda, who I thought was my sister, was in fact my mother. The "special place" I had been dressed to attend was her wedding to my biological father. After the ceremony, I would leave to begin my new life with them.

I hadn't believed Mama when she said I had to leave. I was sure Daddy would make it OK. Hadn't he always made things OK? I knew he loved me way too much to let me go.

The organ was silent now; the vows were said. My new parents approached me and said it was time to go. *Be a big girl*, I told myself, and I was truly trying to be and probably would have been had I not seen Daddy. The eyes that had only beamed with excitement and delight when he looked at me now revealed sadness. Had I done something wrong? What I saw in his eyes overwhelmed me, and I began to sob. I stretched out my arms to him. "Please, don't make me go. Please!" Then, turning to those who were taking me away, I tried bargaining: "I'll give you my hair bows and my black patent leather shoes. Just, please, don't make me go away!"

The next thing I recall is total darkness. I was in a new house, a new bedroom with no sounds, no familiar smells, and no stream of light like the one that flowed from the streetlight outside my other bedroom. Fear engulfed me. I felt so small in such a vast darkness that I was sure at any moment I would forever be lost. Shivering, I pulled the covers up to my chin, but it didn't help. I wasn't shivering from the cold; I was shivering from fear.

Amid the darkness, I could hear something. I listened intently. *Was it Daddy? Had he found me? I knew he wouldn't let me go!* But it wasn't Daddy. It was only a song, one I'd heard before. "Jesus loves me, this I know." I used to sing it while swinging on the front porch at night, serenading Daddy. Many times at song's end, I had giggled in disbelief when Daddy told me that, as much as he loved me, there was someone who loved me even more. *No way,* I recall thinking. *How could that be?*

Now, as an adult, I know my "Daddy" was right. He had planted truth in my heart: There is someone, Jesus, who does indeed love me more than anyone else can. And it was Jesus who made His way through the dark night to a lonely little girl who was about to begin a turbulent and sometimes terrifying journey toward understanding and accepting His great love.

Meanwhile, the pain had begun, the pain no one else knew about. The pain of a four-year-old girl snatched from the only home she had ever known. Literally pulled from the arms of her daddy as tears streamed down his face. That memory evoked such grief and loss that, for many years, I was unable to stumble my way clear of the devastation. So I tucked away that profound hurt deep inside the darkest corner of my heart, marking the beginning of a life full of pretense and masquerade, beginning with a little girl's desire to conform and please; spiraling into a teenager's diet pill addiction, anorexia, and suicidal tendencies; and leading into a young woman's depression and life of lies camouflaged by busyness, social events, and church membership.

The moment you lose who you are, you start to become who everyone else perceives you should be.

My foundation had been shattered on that fall day in Virginia, my safety and security ripped away. I wasn't who I thought I was. I wasn't where I thought I belonged. I began to lose myself in a tumult of unanswered questions. Looking back, I realize the moment you lose who you are, you start to become who everyone else perceives you should be. The moment you lose what you thought you were supposed to do you begin to do what everyone else expects that you should do.

Nothing But a Mistake

One scene from my new life stands out vividly in my mind even today. I had run upstairs to my bedroom to escape the tension and quarrels that were a routine part of life in my new "home." As was my habit, I left the door cracked open just a bit so I could gauge if the argument was escalating or about to settle. The words I heard this night would govern for decades how I would view myself: "If it hadn't been for that mistake, we wouldn't be trapped in this mess." The rest of the argument made me painfully aware I was their "mistake."

Those few words sparked my downward spiral from perceived majesty to a mere mistake. The rejection of my birth parents was much more memorable to me than the simple, unconditional love of my grandparents, who had made me feel like a princess.

The Lady in Gray

Within a few years, my new family had grown to three children. I had a little brother and a baby sister. When I was ten, my dad moved us from Virginia to Mt. Airy, North Carolina, where we lived in a small house across from a cemetery.

During long summer days, I would often sit and watch people come and go from that cemetery. At one burial, my heart went out to the lady in gray who had stayed long after the service ended. I noticed that each day thereafter she came to the graveside and just sat. Her shoulders shook, and I knew she was crying. One day I could stand it no longer. I approached her.

What a sweet lady! Even in her sadness she seemed interested in me. Her smile, her gentle voice, the way she looked into my eyes drew me to her. She asked my name and age, remarked on how pretty I was, inquired about where I lived and went to school. Over the course of several visits, I came to cherish my time with this lady in gray. She didn't seem to care that I was a mistake; she seemed happy that I was there. Eventually I learned that the newly filled grave held her child—a daughter whose life had been claimed in a motorcycle accident. She explained that even though she felt sad about her daughter, she knew she would one day see her daughter again, and that gave her joy.

I understood her sadness, but I could not understand the joy she spoke about. When I asked her about it she whispered to me, "Jesus. He is the one who makes things OK." In subsequent conversations she would talk about how Jesus was helping her, how Jesus was her strength and her calming force. She said He was the reason for her joy and the reason she could smile even in sadness. I thought Jesus sounded like my granddaddy, and I knew they were friends.

She told me that her daughter was now with Jesus, and that He would come one day and she and her daughter would be reunited.

I tried hard to understand. Every time she spoke of having her daughter taken from her I would feel the sting and hurt of being pulled from my grandfather's embrace. I'd see the hurt in his eyes. But as my new friend told me about this Jesus, my heart leaped for joy because He made things OK; He reunited separated people.

I told her about the song I had heard the first night after being torn from my granddaddy. "Jesus loves me, this I know." I described how that song had brought me peace in the midst of the dark, dark night when I had felt so alone. "Is this the same person you speak of?" I naively asked.

"Oh yes," she answered, "but not just a person, Kim. God! And He loves you! He longs to live in your heart, and He wants you to be ready when it is time for Him to come get you."

Come get me! How did she know how desperately I needed someone to come get me—how badly I wanted to be rescued! How did she know? Could she sense the pain? The abuse?

"He loves you, Kim," she repeated, and then she looked toward the sky. "In a moment, in a twinkling of an eye, the trumpet will sound and Jesus will split open the skies and take those in whose heart He lives."

I heard someone else calling my name then, calling in anger. "I have to go," I told the lady. She hugged me tightly and said, "Hurry on, little one. Continue to be a sweet little girl, and always remember Jesus loves you. He'll be coming soon for all His children." That was my last conversation with my nameless friend in gray.

That night, thunder and lightning wakened me from my sleep. No rain fell, but it seemed as if the lightning would rip the sky wide open. The words from my friend at the cemetery came to me: "Jesus is coming back for His children. He will split open the skies." I began to tremble and cry. *Is Jesus coming tonight?* I wondered. Her words seemed to echo from the skies, from the mysterious swaying of the trees, and from the silent gravesites. I grew convinced that this had to be the night Jesus was coming back for His children, and I was not ready. And what was worse, I didn't know how to get ready.

Not until sunrise did I feel safe enough to rest my head upon my pillow. From a little girl's perspective, my endless pleading for Jesus to wait had worked. Unexplainable as it was, I had discovered a new calmness. I was sure everything would be OK. I was completely unaware that my sincere cry was all Jesus had needed to come into my life. *Didn't you have to be in a church to make such decisions? And when would I ever find myself back in such a place to make my decision?* These questions haunted me for a long, long time. I was oblivious to the fact that my name was being written into the Book of Life, and that heaven's inhabitants were in praise because of a sinner's repentance. And I didn't have to know; my incomplete understanding didn't make it any less true.

My lack of understanding, however, caused growing confusion and doubt when my life didn't get better. Had I not been told He would make all things OK again? I could only assume there was more to accepting Jesus than anyone had yet told me. Meanwhile, I had to find some way to survive the continuing abuse and heartache at home.

Send in the Masks

To this day, I can't tell you who taught whom to mask. I can tell you, though, that mask wearing became a way of life, a means of survival for a troubled family in a small community. As we stepped across the threshold of our home into the outside world, we became what the community perceived us to be.

And what was that perception? Well, just count us among your ordinary church-going, choir-singing, all-American families. Mother and Daddy had great careers; we lived in a beautiful home; all three kids were well behaved, academically skilled, and athletically inclined. We were admirable! A family to be respected! An example to follow!

Yet, the inside was very different from the outside. Inside, we suffered silently. If anyone noticed—at church, at school, among the neighbors—it was never talked about. We smiled, we laughed, we did the walkathons and sat in the Bible studies. Outwardly, we did everything that was expected; and then we closed our door to hide the alcohol addictions, domestic violence, abuse, lies, and more. As for me, I appeared to be just your regular straight-A student, Beta Club member, Miss Teen Time, and fun-loving and gregarious cheerleader. Yet I felt alone and confused. Knowing there was another world and I could not participate in it made me wonder if even God had deemed me a mistake. I silently suffered with an addiction to diet pills, anorexia, depression, and life-altering panic attacks.

But no one knew! No one outside the walls of our home had any idea. Or if they did, they never questioned the façade. Not the neighbors we saw every day, not the teachers or other students at school, not the minister with whom we interacted at each of the three church services we attended weekly, not the ladies who sat beside Mother at the office day after day or in Bible study week after week, year after year. They didn't know because we didn't want them to know. We oh-so-proficiently protected the secret. We dressed stylishly, walked confidently, smiled, smiled, smiled, and never but never maintained eye contact for too long. We learned to use body language to intimidate all who dared approach too closely. We manipulated schedules, knew when to change the subject, kept others talking about themselves. Oh yes, we knew how to protect the secret. Time ticked by, and we kept playing our game. Days became years, and the little girl became a teenager and then a woman.

My relationship with Mother was yet another in a series of "performances" in which she and I indulged when necessary. But no matter how cordial our relationship appeared on the outside, at its center was anger and resentment. Time with Mother served only to remind me of a life I believed she had stolen from me. She could have chosen to let me stay where I had been cherished, accepted, and safe. Yet she had watched the hurt; she had seen the tears. Slowly, steadily, the years hardened my heart against this woman for whom I had no respect and less love. My hurt was all her fault.

Me? A Mom?

I had found success in almost everything I undertook: school, career, community service, volunteering. Everything but relationships, that is. I had failed miserably at those. I kept people at arm's length and promised myself I would never again fall victim to love. So how did I find myself married and, soon after, pregnant? I awakened to the reality in horror!

With each of my previous endeavors, I was prepared. I had studied and researched exactly how to achieve "success." But I had no picture of what success looked like for a mother. I knew only one thing: I did not want to be like *my* mother.

I dug out my old early childhood development textbooks. I perused every parenting manual I could find. Nonetheless, I felt utterly unprepared and unqualified to be a mom. Still, the day came. Arriving at the hospital, I was placed on a stretcher and taken to the delivery room. I shivered against the room's cold ugliness. It was old, painted gray, without a whisper of any color or personality. *Funny*, I remember thinking, *it's as though even this room is repulsed at the thought me giving life!*

But I had little time to consider the room's décor or its latent message before my contractions began. When they started, they really started! One hour . . . two hours . . . three, four . . . ten hours later, I heard the shouts. "It's a boy! Ten pounds, six ounces." The nurses immediately nicknamed him Little Hercules.

Everyone bustled about me, yet I felt as if I were in a bubble where everything moved in slow motion. I could hear, but all the voices seemed muted. My eyes found my husband's, and I reveled in Lee's tears of happiness. I saw relief in the doctors' and nurses' eyes. Despite the intensity and length of the delivery, all had ended well. Then, unexpectedly, I felt a precious warmth: Was someone placing this newborn into my arms? But I'd had no time to prepare!

Reluctantly, I held him. Immediately, I loved him.

The once bleak and uninviting room became the most beautiful place on earth as I held my baby Trey. The most incredible, instant, spontaneous, and unconditional love I had ever experienced erupted from deep within my heart. I was astonished at my feelings.

In my peripheral vision, I glimpsed a nurse moving toward me. Surely she wasn't coming to take my baby away? Immediately, I felt myself flexing, holding him ever so tightly. *Not my baby*, I vowed silently. *You will never take my baby from me!*

And then it happened! In an instant, my whole life flooded back, crashing in on my heart. I had been Mother's baby. Until that moment, I never could have understood. I had never known a mother's love. But now, I was living it. My mind raced as my heart tried to catch up with this new truth. "She loved me!" And when confronted with the prospect of someone taking me away, she had also fiercely responded, "No!"

> God had presented me with the truth, and the truth now presented me with a choice.

This truth began its work in my life. Each time I held my precious little guy, I was intensely aware of this new reality. Each time I bathed him, fed him, sat up with him at night, I felt God whisper truths about my mother's love for me. Tiny chip by tiny chip, His whispers chiseled at the hurt that had for so long encased my heart. God had presented me with the truth, and the truth now presented me with a choice: How would I respond? Would I ignore this reality and continue the status quo of anger and unforgiveness toward my mother, or would I accept this truth and pursue what I knew God was asking of me?

While I only allowed others to see the sweet, Southern woman of charm and grace, inside was constant warfare. A heart hardened by hurt tried desperately to come to terms with the past. Day after day, I struggled. Sunday after Sunday, I sat on that pew trying to make sense of it. Bible study after Bible study, I would walk out filled with just as much hurt—and often more personal condemnation—as I had when I entered.

Almost two years passed, and I again found myself pregnant. Everyone seemed to think I had this thing called motherhood mastered, so while secretly distraught with fears I put on my happy face as I announced the "great news."

I had more complications with this baby. Borderline gestational diabetes caused me to gain an unusual amount of weight. But I didn't experience as much anxiety as I had with Trey. I had learned even in the motherhood role to appear skilled and confident.

When the day arrived, I entered the delivery room feeling completely in control of the performance to come. Was it coincidence that the same dreadful décor awaited me even though I was in a different hospital, in a different state? I shrugged off a sense that these walls were a truer reflection of unhappy me than my confident demeanor was.

I was about to learn, however, that my pretense could be shattered within a breath—or should I say, the lack of a breath. For almost as soon as the nurse gave me my baby, and I felt again the stirrings of profound love, that same nurse grabbed him from my embrace. It happened so quickly I had no time to resist. My newborn was snatched from me, gone. Worse, Austin wasn't crying, he wasn't breathing. My son was turning blue! Shouting out codes, the nurse ran from the room with my baby.

Austin would live, but it would take weeks of care in the hospital before he was ready to come home. We could only visit him in the ICU every three hours. Lee and I would travel between home and the hospital around the clock, trying to be there for both boys. It was wearing me down, chipping at my heart. Soon Mother and Daddy came to visit. It was Thanksgiving weekend. I looked at my mom through new experiences and with new eyes. I understood her now, but I wasn't ready to tell her I understood.

God was being very patient with me, allowing me time to sort out my pain and fears. But He knew what I did not know: that time was running out.

A Valentine's Day Miracle

February 14 dawned. I was finally ready to follow the path I felt God wanted me to take. To be honest, I was filled with trepidation. Agonizing memories replayed in my mind of previous overtures to Mother that I had made as a compliant, eager-to-please child— overtures that had been rebuffed. Regardless, I was resolved to move ahead. My plan: send her a dozen red roses and simply sign "Kim" on the card. Never as an adult had I been so gracious in my efforts to reach out to her; therefore, I didn't doubt that she would understand my message. She would know I was seeking her forgiveness. She would know something miraculous had happened in my heart.

With the roses sent, I waited. One hour . . . nothing. Two hours . . . still no word from her. Three, four . . . we did live in different states. Had she received the flowers? Would she call? Was it too late to restore our broken relationship? Could she—would she—forgive me?

Six hours later my telephone rang. Nervously, I picked up the phone. I heard a sweet sob on the other end of the line as she called my name. We had a wonderful conversation! We laughed, we cried, we made plans together. Often forgiveness and reconciliation are a process, but I can attest that God can accomplish them instantly. But then, God knew something that none of the rest of us knew.

One week later, Mother was diagnosed with terminal cancer.

In the weeks that followed, I began to get to know my mother. As I sat by her hospital bedside, holding her disease-stricken hand, I learned about the little girl who had played under the night lights, the preteen who aspired to be an artist. I heard about the abrupt ending of her girlhood dreams with an unplanned pregnancy at age seventeen and the words of condemnation she would never forget. As the cancer ate away at the woman the world had always seen, I was being introduced to the *real* woman—the woman with a heart broken from carrying too many secret burdens.

Mother and I were certain a miracle was on its way. Why would God reunite us just to separate us again? The chemo and radiation treatments were intense, but we kept our hope alive. Day after day I sat beside her, holding her hand as we prayed. We believed.

Then on Easter Sunday morning—nine weeks after her initial diagnosis—Mother was gone, her life on earth over. "Wasted!" had been her assessment. For her entire life, her teenage pregnancy whispered its message of unworthiness, shame, guilt, and regret to her wounded heart. On her deathbed, she agonizingly acknowledged that the successful, poised, and admired woman she had been known as was an impersonation.

Such tears of remorse she cried as death approached! It wasn't that she wasn't prepared; she assured me she had accepted Christ's gift of salvation. Her agony, she explained in some of her last words, was that she had not given her life to Him in *service*. "What will I do, Kim? What will I say?" she cried. "I have nothing to offer Him!" She lamented never having found her purpose. She anguished over having allowed a youthful mistake to cost her a lifelong ministry. Her guilt, lack of personal forgiveness, and concern over what others might think had rendered her useless to her life's calling.

She had attended church, participated in Bible studies, made sure her children grew up in church—yes, she had checked off the list all the little things "church people" do. But beneath this façade of activity, she had lived with a great misconception—and she was dying with it. Mother lived with the notion that once life was better, once her grief and sorrow were gone, once she forgave herself, once her burden had been lifted, *then* she would be useful to God. She never fully understood that there is nothing and no one God cannot use. She never realized that God yearned to use her just as she was.

Little did she know, however, that as the cancer destroyed and disfigured her earthly body, it wasn't too late at all. At the moment Mother spoke her last words of truth to me, God was freed to use her truth, and He used it to begin changing *my* life. God had a lot of work to do, but eventually I would find that same courage to tell my story, and by doing so to pass along Mother's life-changing message to thousands of other women.

The Snooze Button

My mother's death was my wake-up call. But instead of waking up, I hit the snooze button. I determined that no one would see the depth of my hurt after Mother's funeral; they would only see faith in action. I returned to my "proper" life of women's ministry and choir and the other activities that "church people" perform. Looking back, I refer to that period as "my mask through the task." At the time, however, I truly believed that meeting others' expectations was part of what Christian women were called to do.

A single after-church encounter ravaged my composure. I was headed for the produce section of the supermarket, intending to pick up a few items before continuing home as quickly as possible to hide. I had "done my duty" at church and could feel my heart's fault line weakening. Then I heard a familiar voice exclaim, "Kim, I'm so sorry to hear about your mom."

Simple words of condolence, yes, but they affected me differently. Was it the realness with which my friend spoke or her empathy that touched me? To this day I'm not sure. I just know she meant it. She wasn't quoting Scripture, or telling me "time will make it better" or other well-meaning platitudes. Whether it was her eyes truly searching mine, the tone of her voice, her hug, or all of the above, I knew she cared about how I was coping. Racing out of the store, I barely made it to my car before I began sobbing.

> *I emphatically repeated, "Kim, you're OK." But from deep within my soul I heard, No, Kim, you are not OK. But you can be!*

Yes, it was losing Mother that accounted for my grief, but also heaped upon that loss was my fear that somewhere through the years I had lost myself. Mother's last words echoed in my heart: "What will I do, Kim? What will I say? I have nothing to offer Him!" I could see Mother nervously wringing a white linen handkerchief as she lay in that hospital. I could see each tear spill down her face. I could feel her anguish at having allowed a mistake of her early life to cost her a ministry for the rest of her life. I could see her shake her head in disbelief as she recalled how her insecurities had even sabotaged my daddy's efforts to get involved with church. And now, sitting alone in the car, trying to convince myself of its truth, I emphatically repeated, "Kim, you're OK! You are not your mother. You are OK!" But from deep within my soul I heard, *No, Kim, you are not OK. But you can be!*

But could I be OK? Could I believe such a transformation could happen? To others—absolutely! But within me? Not so sure. I needed another wake-up call.

Routine Interrupted

The day of my second wake-up call had started like any other. Outside, the sun glowed as squirrels danced on tree limbs, making the birds scurry from place to place. Inside, my daily routine was unfolding as usual as I prepared to tackle the "must-do" list I had created the evening before.

Dressed and with makeup perfectly applied, I prepared my coffee while noting that I was already running a bit behind schedule because I had overslept. For most of the night my mind had been occupied with the implications of a possible move related to my husband's career. Added to that was the neighbors' dog barking incessantly for what seemed like most all night. That was an item for my list: tell the neighbors what they could do with that barking machine! Other than that my list for the day consisted of routine errands, finding the perfect gift for a friend who "has it all," getting my roots highlighted, and, oh yes, getting those cute red shoes I'd seen earlier to wear to the club Saturday night. Not only would the shoes absolutely complete my outfit; I knew the other women would gush with envy.

With my handbag in one hand and coffee in the other, I was just about out the door when the phone rang. I debated: Do I answer it, or do I just go? Thinking it could be my husband, I threw down my bag and grabbed the telephone.

"Mrs. Crabill, this is your physician's office calling." I settled in for a long phone conversation.

Probable leukemia was the diagnosis. Those words seemed to bring the world to a standstill. The squirrels quit playing, the birds disappeared, and even the breeze that had floated through the oak leaves seemed to hush. And my oh-so-busy schedule slammed to a halt.

I hung up the phone after agreeing to see my doctor the next day. I couldn't believe that just minutes before, my must-do list had held so much importance in my life. A few hours ago I was trying to shake off frustration at a possible move. And now I prayed I would live to make that move, any move.

As I crossed my kitchen I felt as if I were walking through quickly drying cement. *Keep going, Kim, one foot and then another. You have been through worse and survived. Be a big girl. You can do this. Just keep going.* And I did keep going—across the kitchen, up the stairs, counting each step, until I collapsed on the seventh step of 509 Brandermill Road. This is where life had brought me.

The tears burst forth, uncontrollable. Trying to pull myself together, I lifted my head and my eyes rested on the oval mirror hanging from the wall at the bottom of the steps. What did I see? I saw the hurt little girl, now a woman bearing the same secret pain. I saw the truth about all my busyness, all my pretending, all the church work, the cute shoes, the successes—that they were part of a race to outrun that pain. And I saw that I had lost the race.

All my busyness, all my pretending, all the cute shoes were part of a race to outrun that pain.

What I couldn't see at that moment that I now know was that Jesus had begun His journey to 509 Brandermill Road the instant my phone rang that day. He knew the desperation I was about to face. He knew my busyness was about to be halted, my attempts to impress would be stalled, and my running from Him would be over. He knew I was entering a place of truth—not an easy place to be when you've tried all your life to escape the truth. And this Jesus, who had loved me as a little girl lost in the darkness, still loved me and was determined to be in that place with the adult me.

I relived the darkest moments of my life that day. But what my mind was remembering drove me to seek safety, to tuck those secrets away like I always had. After many hours and tears, I reverted to my "pull yourself together" behavior. *I am a big girl now, and I'm ready to go on with life*, I told myself as I rose to my feet. Sure, the threat of leukemia brought me to a new vulnerability. But vulnerability had its limits: Leukemia was one thing; bringing my past to light, as I sensed Jesus urging me to do, was asking too much. I would never surrender to that. I would get through this the way I always got through things: on the run with mask intact.

That being resolved, I made my way down the steps and was rounding the corner into the kitchen when a movement from outside caught my attention. *I guess the squirrels and birds are back*, I thought.

But no. It was the Crabill clan: my husband, Lee, and our two little guys. I affectionately referred to Trey as my "big guy," and Austin as my "little man." Scurrying up the sidewalk they came, Trey hopping and skipping while Austin pulled and tugged from his dad's embrace as if in a hurry. "Mommy, Mommy," they called.

This was my true joy coming toward me. They were my prayers come true—all I had ever truly wanted and prayed for.

And a thought caused me to shiver: Were we, like the family in which I had grown up, another family in crisis? Even though all the circumstances were different, was I not building our lives on the same principles of pretense? Was this the life I wanted to continue modeling for them? Is this what I wanted to leave with my husband and sons?

In those long hours since the leukemia phone call, I had revisited the pain of my past, glimpsed the possibilities of a future lived

Jesus' way, and now before me was the priority of my present. And it was a present I was completely incompetent to deal with as long as I remained the "in-control, make-everything-OK, just-toughen-up-and-get-through-it" woman I had always pretended to be. I needed help, and Jesus had come to me on that stairstep with an extended hand to invite me to run to Him—just as I was.

So many voices were racing through my mind that I wasn't sure I could make sense of them. *Leave me alone . . . Miss Teen Time . . . I can't trust anybody . . . Jesus loves you . . . I'm dying . . . You will have to leave today . . . Mistake . . . Be a big girl . . . Be strong . . . I'm so tired . . . You are not OK, but you can be . . . What will my friends think . . . Probable leukemia . . . What does it matter . . . Things can never change . . . I want to be a good mother for my guys . . . Some things never change . . . Stop! What is the truth? What do I know?*

"Just give me truth," I prayed. I needed truth. I needed clarity. I needed to know.

The words that came to my mind next were my mother's. "I am going to see Jesus, Kim. Any day now I will stand before Him. What will I say? How will I explain I lived my life masquerading as someone instead of accepting the truth and discovering who I was, what I was about, what God had planned for me? Kim, don't live as I am dying; find the life God has for you. Find His plan for you and live it."

Mother had known I was on the same path she had chosen. At the end, she had surrendered to truth. She had chosen to step beyond her insecurity and lack of significance and all the voices that had made her feel inferior and unworthy. Her regret propelled her beyond the threshold of deception and into the presence of truth. And with the articulation of truth, at that very moment, God took a life repressed by the darkness of secrets and miraculously redeemed it and gifted it with purpose.

Standing before the ones I loved that day, I realized I didn't want to resist any longer. I couldn't; the cost was too great. I wanted to be all I could be in the relationships I had been given, and I knew I had to begin with my relationship with Christ. I was ready to surrender my will to His, realign my ways to His ways, exchange my life for the real life He had for me. I didn't have a clue what that meant. I didn't have any answers; I had no plan. I knew I had taken a first step. But what would the next one be? Life as I had known it was again coming to an end, and I didn't even know if I had a future, but I knew whatever time I had left would be focused on what God wanted me to do.

I had been in church long enough to know that God had promised each of us an abundant life (John 10:10). I didn't know exactly what that life looked like, but I *did* know it was not the life I was living. And I knew I was ready to find it. I resolved to move beyond all that had held me back. I had plenty of obstacles to overcome—questions, frustrations, hurts, secrets, walls, façades, fears—but I was determined and committed. I had no clue how my life might change, but I was going to find out! (The leukemia scare later turned out to be a "false positive," but plenty of other life changes were on the way.)

The Rest of the Story

Do you remember Paul Harvey? A radio broadcaster for many years, he sought to bring clarity and insight into the world's situations, beginning each broadcast with those famous words, "And now for the rest of the story." Well, what followed from those hours on the seventh step at 509 Brandermill Road is the rest of *my* story and forms the message of this book and study guide. It is a message that means the world to me—not just because it has transformed my life, and continues to do so, but because it is my mother's legacy. God used my mother's dying confession and insights as a springboard to my own healing and ultimately as a springboard to the healing of thousands of women with whom I've shared my story nationally and internationally.

As we move forward into the coming chapters, I am certain you will discover that you too have a story. Right now it may be a story of pain and trials and heartbreak, but it can become a story of healing and transformation. The burdens you bear today are on the verge of becoming the blessings of tomorrow.

The burdens you bear today are on the verge of becoming the blessings of tomorrow.

Jesus put it this way: "Come to me, all you who are weary and burdened, and I will give you rest" (Matthew 11:28 NIV).

The Greek word for *rest* in this passage is *anapauo*, which means "to refresh by reversal." Jesus does not say bring your burden to Me so I can alleviate or even erase it—either of which He could do if He chose. Rather, He says bring your burden to Me so I can reverse it. Rather than negate all that you have survived, He wants to use it, to turn it around and give it purpose.

The Greek word for *burden* in this verse is *phortion*, and it means "a task or a service-in-waiting." Interesting, isn't it? Have you ever considered that the burden you are carrying is something God is waiting to use? Are you ready for your burden to be reversed from something that weighs you down and holds you back to something that frees you to be of service?

While visiting my freshman son at college some years ago, I could see that he was disheartened by his failure to earn a starting position on the football team; he wasn't even going to travel with the team. Understanding his feelings, his coach looked at me and said, "Austin has great potential. He is going to have a great career. But for now, he is right where he needs to be."

May I pass along that godly coach's encouragement and hope

to you? You are right where you need to be. If like my son, you are feeling sidelined, let me assure you: You have not been forgotten or overlooked. Your Life Coach sees your fears and frustrations, and He knows your potential. He has set all creation in order to get you to this moment, and you are right where you need to be!

By choosing this study you have taken one of the most courageous steps you can take: You have recognized your need and acknowledged that now is the time. You have embraced the wisdom of Ecclesiastes 8:5–6, which says, "The wise heart will know the proper time . . . for there is a proper time . . . for every matter, though a person may be weighed down by misery" (NIV). If the misery of your past is weighing heavily upon you, and you are realizing at last that you are not OK, you are right where you need to be. If your present circumstances have stopped you in your tracks, leaving you paralyzed with fear and frustration, disappointment and disillusionment, you are right where you need to be. If you are contemplating a future that holds more challenges than your faint heart can bear, never mind. You are right where you need to be. If you are ready to offer God all of your life and ask Him to transform your burdens into blessings in ways you cannot begin to imagine, then you are right where God wants you to be!

Keep reading, my friend.

HOW TO PREPARE FOR THE JOURNEY

Maximum results begin with minimum preparations. Here are some ways to prepare for this study and this journey.

1. Prepare your schedule.

Commit yourself to the reading and introspection asked of you. Table whatever other priorities you can. This is your time, and it is too important for you to miss.

Commit to a daily quiet time for study and reflection. It can be five minutes or fifty minutes; I suggest at least thirty minutes. Talk to God, ask Him tough questions, and listen. It is critical that you *schedule* this time, because you will never *find* the time.

Commit to write in your journal daily. Write down what you are thinking, what you are questioning, what you are confused about, what you know God is saying, your prayers, and anything else that might be on your heart.

2. Prepare your space.

Commit a specific space to study. Keep your study guide, your Bible, a pen and/or pencil, note cards, and your personal journal there.

3. Prepare your mind.

Commit to persevering even when you want to give up. Know it will not be easy, but commit to "keep on keeping on." Remember, you have friends surrounding you. Call on them for encouragement. Anticipate great things but have no preconceived notions, thereby freeing God from your ways, your plans, and your priorities.

4. Prepare to study.

Commit to exploring each Scripture to which you feel a connection by asking:

- What does this passage say?
- What does it mean? Is the message literal, symbolic?
- What is the application to my life? What issues does it address?
- What does this Scripture teach me about God?
- What does God want me to learn, change, or do because of this Scripture?

5. Prepare your will.

Commit to doing whatever you sense God is asking you to do—even, or maybe especially, if it costs you. Do whatever it takes to be obedient.

6. Prepare your heart.

There are several ways to prepare your heart for God—thoughtfully reading a favorite psalm or other Bible passage, offering a prayer of dedication, and so on. Music works well for me. The song "Lord, I Offer My Life" is a great reminder that neither I nor my life must be perfect in order to have a purpose.

MAKE IT YOURS
Your Story Begins

Each chapter in this book will include a "Make It Yours" section. Its purpose is to help you process what you've just read and to make it personal. Some questions will help you explore relevant Scripture passages. Others will help you examine your own story for life truths. In fact, as you move forward into the coming chapters, you will discover that you too have a story to tell. These exercises will help that story emerge.

Several questions in each chapter will ask you to interact with the brown bag I told you about in my prologue. If the brown-bag exercises seem awkward at first, bear with me. Each chapter, these exercises will build upon each other and lead to increasing insights into God and yourself. They may become your favorite part of this book!

While my intent is that you be encouraged and built up through these questions, at times you may find the self-examination difficult. That's to be expected; not all memories are pleasant ones. Don't get discouraged. If you need to, skip a question and move on. Understanding yourself and your life experiences through God's eyes unlocks your full potential, but your God is gentle. As you'll recall from my story, He will not drag you kicking and screaming into new insights; rather, He will guide you with tenderness into the kind of self-discovery that brings healing and new life.

I hope you are reading and discussing these chapters with a group of friends. The "Make It Yours" questions can stimulate that group discussion. Some questions, however, may delve into areas too personal or painful to share with a group, especially in the early days of meeting together. You have the freedom to remain silent about those insights you wish to keep private. But don't keep them private from God. Be gut-wrenchingly honest with yourself and Him, even if you aren't ready to share with others. I believe this is what the psalmist means when he writes of God in Psalm 51:6: "You desire truth in the inward parts" (NKJV).

Now, let the processing begin!

1. My story begins with an event at age four that destroyed the foundations of the life I knew. Is there an event from your life that significantly shaped the person you became, whether for your good or your harm? It may not be a dramatic event, and it may not seem all that significant in retrospect, yet it may have powerfully influenced how you came to view yourself.

2. One of the patterns in my story involves pretending to be someone I was not. I call this "wearing a mask" or "masking." Do you think this is something most women do? Why or why not?

3. Have you experienced similar patterns of behavior? If so, describe an instance when you hid behind an acceptable mask instead of being your true self.

4. Why do you think wearing masks is so damaging to our spiritual and emotional growth?

5. Ecclesiastes 8:5–6 says, "The wise heart will know the proper time . . . for there is a proper time . . . for every matter, though a person may be weighed down by misery" (NIV). If you are holding this book, working through these questions, I believe it is because God's "proper time" has come for you. You may not know yet the purpose of this proper time; that may unfold

slowly as you move through this study. But before you go any further, take time to summarize the reason you are reading this book. Maybe a friend gave it to you. Maybe your neighbor coerced you into joining a women's group that was using this book as its guide. Write down how you ended up on this page, answering this question, at this point in your life. It is a marker you will want to remember in the weeks ahead as God begins to transform you.

6. Now it's time to bring out the brown bags. My brown bag, as you read in the prologue, is the representation of the hurts packed away in my heart. As you read this first chapter and answered the above questions, did you discover hidden things tucked away in the brown bag of your heart? If so, what are they? (Remember, you do not need to share your answers with anyone else.)

7. Identifying our hurts is the first step toward discovering what God wants to do with them. The second step is to offer them to God for future blessing. On a slip of paper, write a word or phrase to represent one of the hidden hurts you identified. Now tuck that paper inside your paper bag as an offering to God.

8. I have found that by acknowledging the burdens I carry, I release God to begin His work of transforming those burdens into blessings. Reread Matthew 11:28. How does this passage bring you hope about the burden you carry? Tell God about the slip of paper you have placed in your brown bag as an offering to Him, and ask Him to begin transforming your hurt into hope and your burdens into blessings.

Journal Notes

CHAPTER TWO

Dare to Believe

"Melt Away Ten Pounds in Ten Minutes"
"Learn to Fly in Four Easy Lessons"
"How to Play the Piano . . . Instantly"
"Get Rich Today"

Advertisers' outlandish claims so pervade our culture that we almost universally respond to them with skepticism. But some of God's promises sound equally outlandish, don't they?

"For I am about to do something new.
See, I have already begun!"
—Isaiah 43:19 (NLT)

"Did I not tell you that if you believed, you would see?"
—John 11:40 (NRSV)

"I came that [you] may have life, and have it abundantly."
—John 10:10 (NASB)

Too often, we instinctively respond to God's claims in the same way we respond to telemarketing promises and misleading commercials: we hesitate to believe them.

When I looked into the mirror and heard God promise me a

different future, I was faced with a choice: Would I believe Him or doubt Him? Perhaps you can imagine my internal debate. *God, I've never been OK, so how can You say I will be? Where in the world would I begin to change? How can such a transformation be possible? Sure, it may happen to others. But within me? Not so sure, God!*

From where I stood, the promised abundance seemed a long way off. That God had already begun something new in my life was not easy to see. I couldn't even say to God, "I'll believe it when I see it" because He had strangely reversed that logic in John 11:40, telling me to believe and *then* I would see.

The Power of Believing

God's logic may strike us as mysterious, but research and experience have lent credence to the principle that belief precedes action. Going even further, author and licensed clinical psychologist David Stoop shows in his book *You Are What You Think* that belief *affects* action.

It is not what is occurring in our lives that affects our behavior; it is what we believe about what is occurring that matters. If we focus on the facts related to an out-of-control life, we will behave in a certain matter. If we focus on a life under the control of an all-powerful God, we behave in a different way.

Henry Ford, a titan of industry, said something similar: "If you think you can do a thing or think you can't do a thing, you're right!" And the teacher who wrote the book of Proverbs observed, "For as [a person] thinks in his heart, so is he" (Proverbs 23:7 NKJV).

What you believe really does matter. When you believe you are a failure, you will see every aspect of your life as a failure. When you believe your life will never change, you doom yourself to the status quo. When you believe mediocrity is the best you can do, you'll live a just-get-by existence instead of discovering your potential.

But, dear friends, there is hope! Aligning our thoughts to God's promises provides not only the mental mind-set, but also the motivation we need to move ahead with confidence toward the best that is yet to come. Perhaps that is why God so frequently reminds us in Scripture of the reliability of His promises. Consider these belief-boosters:

> "The Lord your God will bless you as he has promised."
> —Deuteronomy 15:6 (NIV)

> "The Lord always keeps his promises."
> —Psalm 145:13 (NLT)

> "Blessed is she who believed that what was spoken
> to her by the Lord would be fulfilled."
> —Luke 1:45 (NET)

Yeah, But . . .

I bet I know what you're thinking right about now. It goes something like this: *Sure, Kim, it's easy to believe that God is good and in control as long as life looks good and smells good and feels good; but my life isn't like that. Do you expect me to believe God's promises even when hurt and disappointment rule my life? If you ask me, His promises sound a lot like those absurd and misleading advertisements.*

I know how you feel. I have felt the same way. But bear with me a little longer. This is a good place to pause and talk about what belief is.

The word *believe* comes from the Greek word *pisteuo*. It is often translated "faith," specifically "faith to entrust one's well-being to" (*Strong's Exhaustive Concordance*).

Faith, according to Hebrews 11:1, is "being sure of what we hope for, being convinced of what we do not see" (NET). In the Amplified Bible, the same verse reads this way: "Faith is the assurance (title deed, confirmation) of things hoped for (divinely guaranteed), and the evidence of things not seen [the conviction of their reality—faith comprehends as fact what cannot be experienced by the physical senses]" (AMP).

Faith does not mean we deny the burdens we carry. It's just the opposite. Faith gives us the courage and hope to confront our burden—painful, discouraging, even devastating as it is— with the promises of *what it can be*: a blessing. Faith is the pair of glasses we use to see beyond the impossibility of the situation to the assurance that the "impossible" is already accomplished.

The decision to believe God and His reality is the next step to seeing your impossible transformed into all things possible.

Can we possibly believe like that? Absolutely. However, such belief is a choice. It's not an emotion we need to stir up, it's not a quality we can borrow from someone else; it is a very personal choice we each make. And what an effectual choice it is! The decision to believe God and His reality (versus the reality we are living in at the moment) is the next step to seeing your impossible transformed into all things possible.

Abraham and Sarah

Abraham and Sarah, whose story is told in Genesis, are wonderful examples of effectual choice. Their story begins with a promise that looked grossly impossible from a human perspective. Imagine this advertisement in the *Canaan Sun*, the local newspaper of their time:

"Over One Hundred? Wife Barren? No Problem!
Today You Can Conceive a Son!"

Would you have trouble believing such an advertisement? God had promised Abraham a son, yet Sarah was barren. As God spoke to him about his future son, Abraham laughed in God's face. "Will a son be born to a man a hundred years old?" he scoffed (Genesis 17:17 NIV). Was his laugh caused by frustration, years of unfulfilled expectations, a "yeah right" kind of cynicism, anger, or mockery? We don't know. What we do know is that "by faith, even though Sarah herself was barren and he was too old, he received the ability to procreate, because *he regarded the one who had given the promise to be trustworthy*" (Hebrews 11:11 NET).

Abraham and Sarah's childlessness came to an end because Abraham believed God would be faithful to His promises. The circumstances hadn't changed: Sarah was still barren and Abraham was still old. But Abraham decided to put more faith in God than in his circumstances. He chose to answer God's question to Sarah, "Is anything too hard for the Lord? (Genesis 18:14 NKJV) with Luke's later affirmation: "Nothing is impossible for God" (Luke 1:37 CEB).

What about your situation? Are you finding it hard to believe that God can transform your burden into a blessing? I had that same problem, back at Brandermill Road, sitting on that seventh step. I believed a lot of things—we all do—but did I believe the right things? That's where God wanted to help me next.

What's a Girl to Believe?

Remember the description in chapter one of my meltdown after leaving the grocery store? It was shortly after my mother's death, and a woman's expression of sympathy sent me dashing to my car in tears. That's when God spoke His very personal promise to me: "No, Kim, you are not OK, but you can be."

I now had to decide if I could believe Him.

Arriving home that night, I grabbed my Bible and retreated upstairs to a quiet place. I had discovered a passage earlier that I wanted to think about, a passage I eventually came to refer to as one of my "calling Scriptures." It not only spoke to what God wanted to do with my life; it also showed me what I first needed to believe to begin my journey. I've since returned again and again to this passage in order to nail down for myself and for other women what we need to believe about God's character, His ways, and His plan for each of us.

> "This is what God the Lord says—
>> the Creator of the heavens, who stretches them out,
>> who spreads out the earth with all that comes from it,
>> who gives breath to its people,
>> and life to those who walk on it:
> 'I, the Lord, have called you in righteousness;
>> I will take hold of your hand.
>> I will keep you and will make you
>> to be a covenant for the people
>> and a light for the Gentiles,
>> to open eyes that are blind,
>> to free captives from prison
>> and to release from the dungeon those who
>> sit in darkness. . . .
> Former things have taken place,
>> and new things I declare;
>> before they spring into being
>> I announce them to you.'"
>> —Isaiah 42:5–9 (NIV)

Let's dig in and see what these verses can teach us about *what* we can believe in.

(1) Believe in Him.

At its most simple and basic, I believe in "God the Lord" who speaks in this passage from Isaiah. Believing in God—Father, Son, and Holy Spirit—didn't come instantly for me but in stages. This is true of most people. Even Jesus' disciples, who walked and talked and ate and worked alongside Him, had trouble with belief.

> "When they [the women who had discovered the empty tomb] came back from the tomb, they told all these things to the Eleven [disciples] and to all the others. . . . But they [the disciples] did not believe the women, because their words seemed to them like nonsense. Peter, however, got up and ran to the tomb. Bending over, he saw the strips of linen lying by themselves, and he went away, wondering to himself what had happened." (Luke 24:9–12 NIV)

The Life Application Study Bible suggests that a typical Christian experiences four stages of belief.

In stage one, spiritual truth may seem like little more than a fairy tale (or the latest outlandish advertisement) and impossible to believe.

In the second stage, we may be like Peter in the passage above, needing to check out the facts but remaining puzzled by what we discover.

In stage three, we encounter Jesus personally and are able to accept that His promises are true.

In the fourth stage, as we commit ourselves to Jesus and devote our lives to following Him, we begin to fully understand the reality of His presence in our lives.

Where's your "belief barometer"? The fact that you've gotten this far in the study suggests to me that you have gone beyond the fairy-tale stage. Are you in stage two—puzzled and questioning? If so, you are now moving into stage three by encountering

Jesus through the Scriptures within this study. By "encountering" I simply mean you are getting to know Him. Typically, as you get to know Him, your beliefs develop and your faith strengthens. That growing faith leads you to trust Him enough with your life and circumstances to commit yourself to Him, which carries you to stage four where you begin to submit your will to His will in your daily life. As vague and mysterious as that may sound, I have found there's a perpetual discovery and understanding of God's will as I walk with Him, and that day-by-day discovery continues to increase my faith.

I didn't know all that when I first read Isaiah 45, but I did know that—however shaky my faith might be in other matters—the foundation of my belief was in a Person: "God the Lord."

(2) Believe in His power and authority.

Isaiah describes God this way: the Creator of the heavens, who stretches them out, who spreads out the earth with all that springs from it,who gives breath to its people, and life to those who walk on it" (Isaiah 42:5 NIV)

It is one thing to believe that there is a God and He is the Lord. But what we believe *about* God matters too. Isaiah believed in a God of unmatched power and authority. Honestly, I read Isaiah's words, and I must admit I cannot imagine such power. I cannot wrap my mind around it. But with faith, I can let His power wrap around my mind.

Perhaps that is what Abraham did. Romans 4:18 says, "Against all hope, Abraham in hope believed" (NIV). In verse 21, we learn why he could do this: Abraham was "fully persuaded that God had power to do what he had promised" (NIV). Like Abraham, I can choose to be persuaded that the God who created the heavens, spread out the earth, and gave life to everything on earth exercises authority and power over the events and circumstances of my life.

This belief gives me stability when the world seems out of control. It helps me to keep hoping "against all hope."

(3) Believe that His love for you is personal.

Do you understand how much God loves you? Look at the Isaiah passage again and listen to God saying, "I, the Lord, have called you . . . I will take hold of your hand" (Isaiah 42:6 NIV).

Among my favorite memories as a young child are my walks with "Daddy." My little arm could barely reach and hold on to the big hand he would extend to me as we walked. But the security, the sense of belonging, the pure joy it brought kept me holding on long after my arm had fallen numb! That is the image that comes to my mind as I read this passage. And with God, we don't even have to hold on, because as we walk through this life, the hand of the Lord is holding on to us!

Take a moment to reflect on a memory of your own—a time when you felt thoroughly loved and secure. Do you have such a memory? If not, ponder your longing for this kind of love. Let that be a starting place for your belief in God's love for you to grow. I say "starting place" because God's love so surpasses even the best human love that no earthbound memory or longing can quite capture it.

(4) Believe that He is continuously preparing and refining you.

This God of power and authority, this God who lovingly holds our hand, now says, "I will keep you and will make you" (Isaiah 42:6 NIV). (We'll talk about what He will "make" us in a moment.)

I'd like you to think about this: Whatever you are going through, whatever burden you bear—and all of us bear burdens—God is not pacing the carpet of heaven wondering what to do next. He sees the load you carry. He sees your pain and fear and sense of failure, but He sees something more. He sees how all these things are preparing you, are "making" you. And He is keeping you, preserving you even though the hurts of life may at times feel crushing. His hand is *always* and continually on you, as this quote so beautifully expresses: "There is never a moment for the clay when the potter is not doing something with it. God is never standing back and watching us; his fingers are on us all the time."*

(5) Believe He has a plan for you.

What is God making us into? According to His words to Isaiah, He is preparing us "to be a covenant for the people and a light for the Gentiles, to open eyes that are blind, to free captives from prison and to release from the dungeon those who sit in darkness" (Isaiah 42:6 NIV).

These are prophetic words that describe the ministry of the coming Messiah. But they are also words that describe God's plans and purposes for those who follow that Messiah—namely, you and I.

Many of us are caught somewhere between the hurt and the healing. We're still well acquainted with hurt, but we believe in our souls that healing has begun. I suggest that there is a "meantime" between hurt and healing, and God is active and engaged with His plans in that meantime. These words from Isaiah hint at what those plans might look like. Maybe the burdens you bear allow you to reach others with a realness that a burden-free life could not produce. Perhaps your broken heart is keeping you tender toward others who are hurting. Maybe your struggle to break free from a bad habit or addiction will give you the wisdom and patience to help others walk free from personal prisons. Who could be a better bearer of God's hope than one who has experienced it?

Belief in God's greater plan for me has allowed me to look at all situations differently. I've been encouraged even in my sorrow

---

* Austin Farrer, *Said or Sung* (UK: Faith Press, 1960).

by the knowledge that God is working in and through me. He tells us, "Be strong and courageous. . . . Do not be afraid or discouraged, for the Lord God . . . is with you. He will not fail you or forsake you" (1 Chronicles 28:20 NIV). Belief that God has a plan for me has opened my eyes to see unexpected blessings tucked in among some of my painful or unexplainable situations.

> *Belief that God has a plan for me has opened my eyes to unexpected blessings tucked in among some of my painful situations.*

One person whose sorrow God used for blessing is my dear friend and mentor Sandra Aldrich, an author regularly featured on Focus on the Family broadcasts. Sandra lost her husband when their children were very young. She shares this story about her loss and burden in her book[*]:

> During the early weeks of our grief, I was determined that while Jay and Holly had lost their dad physically, they weren't going to lose me emotionally. Every night as I tucked them into bed, I asked if they wanted to talk before we prayed. Sometimes, Jay shared a special memory of his dad or had a question about something at the funeral. But not eight-year-old Holly. She still hadn't cried and kept all of her searing questions inside.
>
> Each evening I continued to ask if she wanted to talk, but she'd shake her head and turn away. Then one night about two weeks after the funeral, she paused, then said, "I do wonder one thing: when we prayed, didn't God listen?"

---

[*] Sandra P. Aldrich, *Will I Ever Be Whole Again? Surviving the Death of Someone You Love* (Enumclaw, WA: Pleasant Word, 2006).

Mentally, I shot a quick prayer for calmness and fresh ideas as I began the hardest explanation I've ever tried to give.

I reminded her of my Grandpa Ted, who had died after his leg was severed in a Kentucky coal mine. He had been only twenty-two years old and had left three children under the age of four. I reminded her of a twenty-eight-year-old man who had been killed at the corner just the week before. His wife was pregnant with a child he would never hold. Then I talked about God's gift to us of those extra sixteen months when the doctors thought her daddy would die within weeks. I added that he could have died with the first cancer when she had been only three years old. When I was talked out, I asked if she felt like praying that night. She nodded, and then began, "Thank you, God, that Daddy died now instead of when I was little."

While Sandra grieved and sought God for answers, to this day she will tell you she doesn't have the answers. But in the same breath, she will tell you that she got up and kept going—and in doing so, she lives out God's plan of blessing. She writes books, speaks at conferences, and has been called upon to use her grief to help others who have lost loved ones.

Many times we simply do not and will not understand what God is doing. The more we struggle to understand, the more confusing the situation can become. Our part is to remember He truly has a plan for us. Armed with such resolve, we can then acknowledge God's control and be assured He can use even seemingly random and chaotic events to complete His plan and ultimate blessing for us. We have to decide if we are willing to trust God and continue on with our life of purpose, as Sandra has done.

(6) Believe He will reveal His plan to you.

Hear God speaking to Isaiah—and to us: "New things I declare; before they spring into being I announce them to you" (Isaiah 42:9 NIV).

This Scripture takes me back to that night as a four-year-old, removed from my home, petrified by the deep darkness of a strange bedroom. With not a glimmer of light to be seen, I felt I was about to be lost forever to darkness.

Many times in life I have felt such darkness. I couldn't figure out what God was doing or how He could bring anything good from the situation. Have you ever known that darkness—when you're lost in despair and confusion, perhaps because of your own foolish sin and mistakes, or when relationships break or a loved one dies or a medical diagnosis leaves you reeling? In these times, there seems to be no plan. Yet this Scripture is our hope. It assures us that God not only has a plan for us but He also promises to reveal that plan.

Our God is a God who speaks. Later in this book, we'll discover how to sensitize our ears and our hearts to His voice. But first, we must believe He is a God who wants to reveal Himself and His plan to us. Here is a belief-boosting practice for you to adopt: as you read through your Bible—in the coming weeks, months, years—pay attention to all the times and ways that God spoke. He once spoke through a donkey! This tells me that God will go to great lengths to communicate with His people.

(7) Believe that He believes in you.

"Former things have taken place," says God, through His prophet Isaiah (Isaiah 42:9 NIV).

This may be my favorite part of all, because as I read these words, it's as if God is saying to me, "I know all about your past! It is done. The past is history; that is where it needs to remain—in the past! I'm going to do something new."

How freeing! And how amazing! Remember who is speaking here: God the Lord—"the Creator of the heavens, who stretches them out, who spreads out the earth with all that springs from it, who gives breath to its people, and life to those who walk on it" (Isaiah 42:5 NIV). This same God sees me, knows me, holds my hand, and guides me. This God unconditionally loves me *and* believes in me. Believes in me enough to say, "Keep going; I'm offering you a brand new day." How amazing is that! He knows my past—every mistake, regret, doubt, how I was abused, how I abused—and He still finds me worthy.

I'm reminded of when Trey and Austin were learning to walk. As a parent, I had no doubt they would learn to walk eventually. Yet as they went from crawling to pulling themselves up on the tables, I was always there to cheer them on. As they began to let go and stumble toward a step, falls were inevitable. Yet I smiled and clapped and exclaimed, "Good job!" Looking back, I wonder if they thought Mommy was foolish to be making such a big deal about them lying there flat on their faces! Many falls would come before they mastered the art of walking and then running. But I never doubted them. I always believed in them.

God looks at your past, and then He turns His attention to how He's going to transform that past into your promising future.

Wherever you are, wherever you have been, God has no doubts about your future. He believes in you. Still! He has not reviewed your past and declared you unfit for service—though you may have declared yourself unfit. He is not discouraged by that fall you took today, because He is focused on your potential. He looks at your past, and then He turns His attention to how He's going to transform that past into your promising future.

Few stories illustrate this truth better than that of the Samaritan woman.

A Woman and a Well

The Samaritan woman's life unfolds for us in John 4. Everything seems to be stacked against her. Being a Samaritan was not too cool in her time—today we might say she was from the "wrong side of the tracks." Being a woman wasn't so great either. To add to her unfortunate lot in life, she had made a slew of poor choices that had left her with five ex-husbands and, as this account begins, a new live-in boyfriend.

Picture the Samaritan woman coming to draw water from a well. Jesus is sitting there, and He begins talking to her.

"Will you give me a drink?" . . .

The Samaritan woman said to him, "You are a Jew and I am a Samaritan woman. How can you ask me for a drink?" (For Jews do not associate with Samaritans.)

Jesus answered her, "If you knew the gift of God and who it is that asks you for a drink, you would have asked him and he would have given you living water."

"Sir," the woman said, "you have nothing to draw with and the well is deep. Where can you get this living water? Are you greater than our father Jacob, who gave us the well and drank from it himself, as did also his sons and his livestock?"

Jesus answered, "Everyone who drinks this water will be thirsty again but whoever drinks the water I give them will never thirst. Indeed, the water I give them will become in them a spring of water welling up to eternal life."

The woman said to him, "Sir, give me this water so that I won't get thirsty and have to keep coming here to draw water."

He told her, "Go, call your husband and come back."

"I have no husband," she replied.

Jesus said to her, "You are right when you say you have no husband. The fact is, you have had five husbands, and the man you now have is not your husband. What you have just said is quite true." (John 4:7–18 NIV)

Scripture tells us that Jesus had made His way to this woman on this day. Why? He knew the depth of her depression. He knew the cruelty of others' words and the ridicule she had endured. He knew how men had taken advantage of her. Does His continued prodding suggest to you that He had come to deliver more of the same condescension and judgment?

If the account ended there, you might be justified in imagining so. However, as the story continues we see Jesus again reaching out to her: "I am he [the one who offers the living water]" (John 4:46 NIV).

Despite, or perhaps because of, her past—the past that had previously offered a lifetime of shame, guilt, and regret—Jesus had made His way to her to offer a new way of life. He knew the time had come for Him to reverse her curse and pour out His blessings. "Instead of shame and dishonor, you will enjoy a double share of honor [blessing]" (Isaiah 61:7 NLT). Jesus' continued prodding of the Samaritan woman was simply to bring her to the truth about herself. He had not been fooled by her masks. He knew all there was to know about this woman, but He also knew that only as she acknowledged and confessed the depth of her sin to Him—and the condemnation she and others had heaped upon herself— would she be able to recognize and accept His unconditional love and blessing for her. Only then would this hurting, unloved social outcast be able to set aside her questions and declare with confidence, "Jesus loves me, this I know."

Years after he wrote about the Samaritan woman's encounter

with Jesus, the apostle John penned these words: "This is how we know what love is . . . and how we set our hearts at rest in his presence: If our hearts condemn us, we know that God is greater than our hearts, and he knows everything" (1 John 3:16, 19–20 NIV).

John C. Maxwell has written, "Believing in people before they have proven themselves is the key to motivating people to reach their full potential." Jesus believed in the Samaritan woman. He had come to reveal the plan He had for her life. And because this woman believed in Him and His plan, Jesus accomplished an amazing transformation within a woman others had written off as insignificant and unworthy:

> The woman went back to the town and said to the people, "Come, see a man who told me everything I ever did." . . . They came out of the town and made their way toward him. . . . Many of the Samaritans from that town believed in him because of the woman's testimony . . . They said to the woman . . . "We know that this man really is the Savior of the world." (John 4:28–30; 39, 42 NIV)

Only Jesus could have known, throughout this woman's years of torment and pain, that the time would come when shame would haunt her no longer. Instead, every hurt, every regret, all the days of public ridicule and mockery would become something God used to enhance her personal ministry and demonstrate His all-encompassing love and acceptance for any and all who would just believe.

The story of the Samaritan woman bears out God's truth that He meets us right where we are, wherever that may be, but He doesn't leave us there. He has a plan for the burdens we carry—He has a plan for *us*. I am praying you will come to see this book as God's way of coming to you—right where you are—and that you will take His hand and let Him lead you into that plan.

Do you dare to believe?

It's Already Purchased

Christmas is one of my favorite holidays. Just ask anyone who knows me. My poor boys never had the chance to wake me on Christmas morning to open their packages because I was already awake and waiting for them! I loved seeing their faces light up when they realized they had received what they wanted. Oh yes, I had purchased most of the items when they had asked, but their gifts had been locked away in the closet until the time was right. The boys couldn't see them, but the gifts were already there. Many times I would act as though their requests were impossible to fulfill, but then I had to bear the disappointment those precious little faces so gallantly tried to conceal. It was heart-wrenching for me, knowing the gifts were already bought and paid for but having to withhold them from my boys until Christmas. But what delight Christmas morning brought when I could finally present the gifts and see my boys' happiness!

In Luke 11:11–13, God asks:

> "Which of you fathers, if your son asks for a fish, will give him a snake instead? Or if he asks for an egg, will give him a scorpion? If you then . . . know how to give good gifts to your children, how much more will your Father in heaven give . . . to those who ask him!" (NIV)

If I think I know how to make my boys happy, can you imagine what God is up to? And our blessings are already bought and paid for! We cannot see them yet; they may still be hidden in the closet. But they will arrive at the perfect time, often in the most ordinary of daily circumstances. Believe it!

Faith Fighters

Sometimes, no matter how clear the Scriptures are, no matter how clear the evidence of God's good character and loving plan for us, belief eludes us. Doubt sets in, and it can be crippling. I explained it this way in a magazine article I wrote a few years back:

Doubt, if not confronted, has the devastating potential to lead us down the path of dejection and despondency. This is how: Many times, doubt and discouragement erupt during the "meantime" of our spiritual journey. This is the way I have experienced it. In a quiet moment God highlights a promise that meets my need as I am striving to fulfill a role or be obedient where He has placed me. Often, He seals these words with confirmation, and then He seemingly steps away. During this quiet and sometimes dark time, He allows the tempter to come in. Circumstances, opportunities, others' responses, and even my own thoughts may seem to contradict all that He has spoken. This is my time to become a faith-fainter or a faith-fighter. Which I become is totally dependent on what I choose to believe.

Doubt will inevitably enter your mind. Expect it! But it does not have to affect your *actions*. "Fight the good fight of the faith," Paul wrote to his protégé, Timothy (1 Timothy 6:12 NIV). We fight for our faith by fighting against doubt. And we fight against doubt by feeding our faith. I have found several effective ways to do this. Maybe some of them will work for you.

Pray. When believing is a challenge I don't depend on myself. I ask Jesus to help me. That's what the demon-possessed boy's father did when he needed to believe in order to see his son healed. He beseeched Jesus, "I do believe; help me overcome my unbelief" (Mark 9:24 NIV).

Walk through Hebrews. To remind myself of how God has worked out His promises in so many lives, I read the wonderful testimonies in Hebrews 11.

Recall your own God stories. There are times when I simply know, without a doubt, that God showed up for me or a family member or friend. If He can do it once, He can do it again—and

He has. When my faith falters, I remind myself of how God acted on my or a loved one's behalf in the past and what blessings unfolded as a result.

Hold your thoughts accountable. During times of doubt, we need to "take captive every thought to make it obedient to Christ" (2 Corinthians 10:5 NIV). Doubting expresses itself in different ways. For me, it might say, "What's the use?" or "God doesn't care." When I hear these and similar messages, I can isolate that thought and make it obedient to Christ by putting His truth to it. For example, if my thoughts tell me "God doesn't care," I can remind myself of 1 Peter 5:7: "Cast all your anxiety on him because *he cares for you*" (NIV). When doubt leaves me feeling lost and uncertain and not knowing what to do, I personalize the truth of James 1:5: "If I lack wisdom, I should ask God and He will give generously."

Memorize God's truths. I memorize whatever scriptural truths I find to confront or replace my doubts and negative thinking. That way, when the "stinking thinking" and lies begin, I can choose to intervene immediately by replacing my thoughts with God's thoughts.

Over time, you will probably add some "faith fighters" of your own to this list. Remember, though doubts will invade your mind, God has not left you unarmed and defenseless in the fight for your faith. And with each battle you fight, your doubts will diminish and your faith will grow stronger.

Be Daring!

Some of you are reading about applying biblical promises to the lies you tell yourself—or memorizing verses that confront negative thinking—and your response is, "I don't know where to begin. I don't know my Bible well enough to do any of that!" That's OK. Until God gives you applicable Scriptures for your particular situation, use this one to direct your thoughts: "Finally, brothers and sisters, whatever is true, whatever is noble, whatever is right, whatever is pure, whatever is lovely, whatever is admirable—if anything is excellent or praiseworthy—think about such things" (Philippians 4:8 NIV).

> *It is not what is actually occurring in our lives that affects our behavior, but rather what we believe about what is occurring.*

When events appear to defy what you know to be true about God and His posture toward you, this verse can be a starting place for boosting your faith and reminding you to look for the right kind of truth to live by. Remember it is not what is actually occurring in our lives that affects our behavior, but rather what we believe about what is occurring.

Your decision to begin this study speaks to your readiness for growth and change, to grasp God's special plan for you—only you. It speaks to your readiness to believe that a new beginning is possible, one full of grand opportunities. God has promised that by His mighty power at work within you, you can accomplish infinitely more than you could even ask or dare to imagine (see Ephesians 3:20)! Do you believe—really believe—this promise? If you don't, you can. At least, that's how it was for me.

I walked countless steps, battling godless thoughts and personal demons, as I fought through to a deeper faith that would open my eyes to the truth of what God had said to me. "I could be OK!" Looking beyond the obvious reflection in my mirror that day, I saw the image of a little girl, still four years old, with long blonde hair and sad blue eyes and holding a suitcase. Long ago, she had become stuck in her hurt. As the outside matured, the little girl stayed hidden away—always hurting, crying, waiting. All efforts to ease the pain—being good enough, smart enough, skinny enough—proved to be empty fixes that left the little girl desolate and confused. She adopted a life of masquerade and disguise. But just as with the Samaritan woman, Jesus knew not only how to reach that little girl's hurt but how to heal and bring it purpose. Just as He knew the Samaritan woman needed to hear the words, "I can offer you living water," He knew that girl in the mirror needed to hear the words, "You can be OK."

I don't know what your burden is, but God does. And what God promised me, He also promises you. Read that promise again, but insert your name this time:

> Glory be to God, who by his power working within
> _____, _____ can accomplish abundantly more
> than _____ could even ask or dare to imagine!

Dare to believe! Author and theologian Thomas C. Upham gives this challenge: "Be willing to live by believing; but neither think nor desire to live in any other way."* Allow your belief to propel you toward your promised blessing. I don't know how God plans to bless you and use you to bless others, but I know He will reveal it to you. He believes in you. He wants to heal you. He wants to use you, to give you a life of purpose. These things are all part of your blessing, and the next step for you to take toward that blessing is to believe. What is God saying to you? Take to heart these words from Paul, who had his share of struggle and pain and burdens to bear: "Keep up your courage . . . for I have faith in God that it will happen just as he told me" (Acts 27:25 NIV).

---

* Thomas C. Upham, *The Life of Faith: In Three Parts* (New York: Harper & Brothers, 1856), 151.

MAKE IT YOURS
Stepping Toward Belief

Just a reminder: please answer these questions knowing that you need not share anything until you are ready. This exercise is for your private, personal use.

1. What are some really outrageous commercials or ads you've seen that promise the impossible?

2. Let's look at what some may consider "Scripture ads." Write a headline for each verse that summarizes what God is offering His "target audience."
   - Isaiah 43:19
   - John 10:10b
   - Deuteronomy 15:6
   - Ephesians 3:20
   - Romans 8:28

3. Think back to your brown bag and the burden you put there at the end of chapter one. Do you believe God can bring anything good from this burden? Or do these promises seem like "false advertising" based on your past experience? On a scale of 0–10 (0 being no belief and 10 being absolute belief), where would you place yourself?

4. Of the three stories in this chapter—mine, Sarah's, and the Samaritan woman's—which bolsters your belief the most? Why?

5. This chapter identified seven key beliefs from Isaiah 42. Which, if any, of these beliefs do you already hold with confidence?

6. Which of these beliefs is hardest for you to embrace? Why do you think that is?

7. What comfort do you find in Hebrews 4:14–16 regarding your struggle to believe?

8. Take a moment to reread Ephesians 3:20. Does it sound like false advertising, too good to be true? Or are you starting to get a glimpse of the God behind the promise, the God of Isaiah 42? Will you dare to believe that God can take your bagged burden and transform it into blessing beyond what you can even imagine? Show your commitment to this belief by pulling out your paper bag and writing your personalized declaration of Ephesians 3:20 on the back of your bag. When your inner voice tells you, *This is impossible; my burdens will never change*, let this verse be the truth that replaces that lie. Dare instead to believe that God is able to do a new thing in your life.

Journal Notes

CHAPTER THREE

Seize God's Timing

Now is the time.
—2 Corinthians 6:2 (NIV)

In chapter one I shared how, for many years, I carried heavy burdens that kept me from being honest with myself, God, and other people in my life. Those burdens—and my compulsion to hide or deny the pain they created—kept me from experiencing life at its fullest, life as God intended it to be. I suspect you still hold this book in your hands because you can relate to my story.

In chapter two, having acknowledged our burdens, we looked at the next step toward a more meaningful life: belief. We saw how essential it is to believe what is true—about ourselves, about God, and about our burdens. And we looked at some ways to begin growing in belief or faith.

Now it's time to dig even deeper. We're about to discover that once we begin to acknowledge the truth and peel away our masks, God steps in with perfect timing.

A Time for Everything

There is a time for everything,
and a season for every activity under heaven:

a time to be born and a time to die,
a time to plant and a time to uproot,
a time to kill and a time to heal,
a time to tear down and a time to build,
a time to weep and a time to laugh,
a time to mourn and a time to dance,
a time to scatter stones and a time to gather them,
a time to embrace and a time to refrain from embracing,
a time to search and a time to give up,
a time to keep and a time to throw away,
a time to tear and a time to mend,
a time to be silent and a time to speak,
a time to love and a time to hate,
a time for war and a time for peace.
—Ecclesiastes 3:1–8 (NIV)

A profound truth emerges from this passage. God has all things planned, and He is in total control. He unfolds His plan even in the midst of our sins and poor choices and the horrific tragedies life can bring. He is forewarning us, yet again, as He did in John 16:33, that our lives will be filled with ups and downs, good and bad, mourning and dancing, tragedy and triumph. But God's final word is always our hope. Ecclesiastes 3:11 promises: "He has made everything beautiful in its time" (NIV).

This becomes our hope: The best is yet to come. God's blessings are on their way! And this becomes our challenge: we can't give up!

Still, understanding God's timing is imperative to reaping God's blessings. Why? Because we live each day according to His very precise timeline, not ours.

Verse 2 of Ecclesiastes' third chapter defines the boundaries or this timeline—the bookends of your life: "A time to be born and a time to die" (NIV). For everyone, there is a beginning breath and a concluding breath. Just as surely as you and I have already experienced the first, our last is on its way. This is not a morbid statement; it is a fact. God has set those dates, and they will not be changed.

Think of what is inscribed into a headstone.

Linda L. Sawyer
August 14, 1938 – January 21, 2001

What do you see? A name, a beginning date, an ending date. Yes, but what else? Nothing? Look again. Oh, yes . . . that dash! That tiny dash represents ups, downs, good days and bad days, moments in the sun and moments of extreme darkness. It can just as well represent the brevity of which the Bible speaks:

Show me, O Lord, my life's end and the number of my days; let me know how fleeting is my life. . . . Everyone is but a breath. (Psalm 39:4–5)

Fleeting, yes, but that dash is a powerful symbol of a moment in time—your moment in time. One day, your dash will represent how others remember you, how they were affected by who you chose to be. It will depict your choices—to forgive, to accept, to care, to love—choices far more consequential than the color of your nail polish or the size of your clothing or the number of your wrinkles.

Ecclesiastes 3:2 begins with those things over which we have no control: our time to be born and our time to die. But between those two events—the dash—we make our choices, live out our purpose, and leave our legacy. Our times to weep, mourn, search, be scattered, laugh, dance, mend, and heal will unfold in different seasons of our lives. Knowing peace is coming helps us get through the battles; understanding that healing is on the way can light the path through the dark and lonely times. But unlike the appointed times of birth and death, many of these events may be dependent upon our discovery, acceptance, understanding, and seizing of God's timing.

Seizing God's Timing

When we think about God's timing, it's usually in terms of *waiting* on God's timing. I challenge you to redirect your thinking to *seizing* God's timing. I shared with you my story about reconciling with Mother so that you could see how different my life would be today had I waited just one more week to reach out to her. How differently my motive may have been perceived just seven days later, once her cancer was diagnosed!

Certainly waiting on God's timing can be vitally important; indeed, the Bible regularly admonishes us to wait for God and is replete with examples of trouble that arose from restlessness and haste. Waiting requires enormous personal endurance and perseverance. But there is another side to God's timing, which author and pastor James Russell Miller identifies:

> We cannot wait for the fruit to ripen, but insist on plucking it while it is green . . . We cannot wait for the answer to our prayers, although the things we ask for may require long years in their preparation for us. We are exhorted to walk with God; but ofttimes God walks very slowly. But there is another phase of the lesson: God often waits for us.[*]

While it is true we may risk many blessings by not waiting on God, it is also true that we may jeopardize just as many, and possibly more, of His blessings by over-waiting. Sometimes we must "seize" His timing. Sometimes we are meant to move forward with a strong resolve.

---

[*] J. R. Miller, *Things to Live For* (New York: Thomas Y. Crowell & Co., 1896), 167–68.

Sometimes we are meant to move forward with a strong resolve.

While writing this chapter I got into a pattern of write, crumple, and toss. Write. Crumple. Toss. I was sure it was God's time for me to write down what He had been teaching me and, through me, teaching others. Yet the process seemed thwarted. I began to wonder, *What is God up to?* After four days of this draining exercise, I was about to throw up my hands in defeat when something rather incredible happened. At about six o'clock, my cell phone rang. On the other end was Linda, a distant yet longtime friend. We instantly rekindled a friendship, suspended nearly two years earlier, by catching up and giggling at old times.

During our conversation, Linda reminisced about all the things we had learned together years earlier in a Sunday school class I had taught. She confessed, "I have wanted to call you for so long just to say thank you. And today as I was riding up the road, I heard a little inner whisper, 'Now. Now, Linda, is the time!'"

Bells and sirens sounded in my mind! I nearly shouted in triumph and understanding! Linda's obedience, unknown to her, was the next step in my writing, the resolution to my internal turmoil. Of course I had enjoyed and appreciated her call, but God had a larger plan. In the midst of writing a chapter about waiting for God's timing, I was interrupted by God Himself, who revealed that my continued disquiet (all that crumpling and tossing!) had to do with the fact that I was delivering the wrong message altogether. He sent Linda to convey His intended message: "Now is the time. You have hit the snooze button long enough. You know what to do. You have been waiting, but now is the time!"

But you may be asking, "Time for what?"

The Next Small Step

In the last chapter, we saw that the transformation of our burdens into blessings begins with the small step of belief. It's dangerously easy, however, to stop there. We settle for believing that God has a plan for us, but we don't move toward that plan in obedience. We just relish the *idea* of it.

But if we are going to realize God's blessings in our lives, we have to continue taking steps toward what He says we should do. I believe it's time to take the next step, which begins with this question: What do you know you are supposed to do but haven't found the requisite courage or time to accomplish?

Here's the thing: We've established that God has plans for you, plans that are undergirded by promises He extends to you. But many divine promises are conditioned upon some beginning action on your part. As we step out in obedience, God blesses.

Remember Abraham? Not one of the promises God had made to him would have been fulfilled had he not first stepped out of the comfort of Chaldea. Abraham had to leave home, friends, and country, venture down unknown paths, and press on in unfaltering obedience through famines, family problems, and even battles to receive his promised blessing. While I doubt God is calling you to such extremes, I'm sure you'll be challenged to step beyond your comfort zone.

Do you dare to see what God has waiting for you? It will be unknown territory, and don't expect it to be easy to navigate. You may have to leave the comfort of family and friends' understanding. You may have a few personal battles to fight along the way. But what God promised to Abraham He continues to promise to you and me today. Despite what has happened to us in the past, what burdens we carry, He says, "I will bless you . . . and you will be a blessing" (Genesis 12:2 NIV).

As you step out, you'll have all kinds of questions. How?

When? What? How long? Without guaranteeing any answers, God simply directs: "Be strong and courageous, do not be afraid or terrified . . . [because] the Lord your God goes with you; he will never leave you or forsake you" (Deuteronomy 31:6 NIV). And this same "God who gives life to the dead . . . had power to do what he had promised" (Romans 4:17, 21 NIV).

If God promises He will be with you—and He does—then He will! And if He promises He will bless you—and He does—then He will!

No Spiritual Wand

Am I making you a little uncomfortable? I hope not—that is certainly not my intent. But I feel I can be this challenging, this "in your face," because I know how long I was stuck between hurting and healing and how hard it was for me to seize God's timing and move toward His promised blessing. If you are also stuck or stumbling around in the darkness, I want to come alongside you and encourage you—even at the risk of being a little bold. You see, I believe God has a plan designed just for you, and I don't want you to miss it and the blessing it will bring to your life,

When I first heard those words, "You are not OK, but you can be," I think I expected God to wave some kind of "spiritual wand" and suddenly it would happen: I would be OK. It didn't immediately enter my mind that I had a lot of work ahead of me. I didn't understand then that I had to take some very practical steps of obedience. I needed someone to be a bit "in your face" with me! And as you'll read later on, I needed friends to come alongside me for motivation and advice.

At a point in my journey when darkness seemed to be prevailing, I stumbled upon Psalm 119:105: "Your word is . . . a light for my path" (NLT). I slowly began to understand. God's truth shines the light onto the path, but I have to choose to walk that path. I can't just stand in place and admire it. I had to begin my part of the work, and years later I'm still working toward being what God has created me to be. Have you seen those wristbands that say "PBPGINFWMY"? It stands for "Please be patient, God is not finished with me yet." Believe me, those words could have been written about me! But at least I'm on the path and moving forward. I am not completely where I want to be in my spiritual journey, but thanks be to God, I'm not where I used to be. My waiting is over; I've seized God's timing.

Back to the Well

Let's return to the Samaritan woman from John 4. There we find a significant insight into where our obedience to God's timing begins.

When Jesus made His way to that well in Samaria, He knew the woman would be there. He knew her brokenness, her anguish, her guilt, and her shame; He understood her anger, her resentment, and her abandoned dreams. And He knew something no one else, not even the woman, knew. He knew the plan He had for her, and He knew this was her time.

When He offered this woman "living water," I wonder what she imagined that to be. Perhaps her first hope was for an easier life. Home delivery of living water! No more daily treks to the well to face vulgar comments and accusatory looks. Good thought, but no. Jesus had come to offer so much more! He wanted to take the only "water" she had to offer—all that she considered vile, regretful, abusive, and wasteful—and gift it with meaning and a purpose, if she would allow Him. He had come—at the perfect time—not to take away the life she had already endured, but to bring significance to it.

Here's a secret you don't ever want to forget: the starting place for the Samaritan woman that day, and still for us this day, is the place of truth. If you read their dialogue carefully, you'll see how Jesus kept taking her back to the truth of her life—not to condemn her, as had the townspeople, but to free her. When confronted with that truth, however, she was also confronted with the change it brought—and with a choice!

The Truth Shall Set You Free

Jesus makes a bold claim in John 8:31–32: "If you hold to my teachings, you are really my disciples. Then you will know the truth, and the truth will set you free" (NIV). In other words, if you know Christ—if you follow Him—you will be able to discern His truth and know the way through those things that hold you captive to hurt, despair, fear, unsettledness, addictions, abandoned dreams, whatever is stealing your peace and joy. But here is the clincher: The truth that sets you free is the truth about you. Not about anyone else. Jesus loves you enough to make it all about you!

> The truth that sets you free is the truth about you.

Yes, the Samaritan had been hurt by others; Jesus knew she had been mistreated, abandoned, and abused. But Jesus hadn't come to talk about those who had hurt her. Jesus came to talk about her and His particular plan for her.

That conversation is not an easy one to have. Ever. Yet the Samaritan woman seized God's timing by listening to what Jesus had to say, by believing that He spoke the truth, and then by stepping out beyond her comfort zone in obedience. "Then, leaving her water jar [a representation of all that bottled up despair] the woman went back to the town and said to the people, 'Come see a man who told me everything I ever did!'" (John 4:28–29 NIV).

I hope you will stop and let these verses sink into your heart. This is an incredible picture of what an encounter with Jesus Christ can do not only inwardly but also outwardly. This astonishing woman returned to the same circumstances, the same problems, the same reputation, the same five ex-husbands, the same live-in boyfriend, the same townspeople who had used and shunned her—but something was different: She was! She had met a Man who had shown her the truth about herself and then given purpose to her life.

That's what God can still do for you today.

The Role of Relationship

I can't imagine reading a story like that of the Samaritan woman and not saying, "That's what I want! I want a transformation of all those things I've endured! I want my life to be used by Jesus!" But another question comes to mind: "How do I know if I'm supposed to wait or act? And if I'm over-waiting and need to act, what action am I supposed to take?"

I remember when Trey, my firstborn, was only a few months old and very "unhappy." Colicky? Spoiled? All I knew was that he cried all the time, and I didn't have a clue what to do. So off to the experts we went. "What is wrong with this child?" we asked. Their response: "Either you are underfeeding him or you are overfeeding him." Can you imagine my frustration?

In the end, it came down to this: only I could know what was causing Trey to be cranky, because I was the one with a relationship with him. I had to try more food, then less, and watch how he responded. It was a process I had to initiate. With each action step, I came closer to conclusions and answers, until eventually I knew exactly how to respond to my son.

I submit that finding God's timing and plan for healing the burdens you carry—and showering you with the blessings you have yet to receive—will come only through your relationship with your Father. You can consult all the experts of the day. You can read the self-help magazines. You can even have your palms read. But Paul cautions us, "See to it that no man takes you captive through hollow and deceptive philosophy, which depends on human tradition and the elemental spiritual forces of this world rather than on Christ" (Colossians 2:8 NIV).

Paul, the gifted philosopher of the Bible, is not condemning philosophy with this verse; he simply understands that the world's timing, solutions, and ideologies do not have the power to heal our broken hearts and our broken lives. Only Christ does. And Christ works through relationship.

Do you want to hear what God is saying to you? If so, you must listen for His voice. How will you recognize His voice? By staying close enough in your relationship with Him that you can tell His voice apart from all others.

My youngest son, Austin, loved roaming the neighborhood when he was a little guy. Sending him out to play, I would admonish, "Stay close so you can hear Mommy when I call you at dinnertime." Austin had great intentions to obey; however, his gregarious personality combined with enticing invitations from his friends would cause him to wander past the range of my voice. When it was time for him to come home, he couldn't hear me. I think of this so often when I feel as if I'm not hearing from God. I'm sure He has a lot to say, but have I been enticed beyond my spiritual "hearing range"?

Hearing Him is possible. We know this because John 10:27 says, "My sheep hear my voice" (KJV). So how do we hear God?

Prior to caller ID technology telling you in advance who was calling you on the phone, how did you recognize your callers? If it was someone you knew well, had spent a lot of time with, had talked to many times before, then you recognized her voice before she even told you her name, right? You didn't need to see her face. You didn't need the help of technology. You knew, because you had a relationship with her.

Similarly, we learn to recognize God's voice as our relationship with Him grows. You may not be able to see His face, you may not have heavenly caller ID, but if you've spent time in His presence, talking with Him, listening to Him through what He says in His Word, you will soon discover that His voice is a familiar one. This is the God who says, "I have called you friends" (John 15:15 NKJV). Hearing God is a matter of developing a friendship with Him.

Here are some ways I've found to nurture my friendship with God.

Just as you would with a friend, **meet regularly and often.** Many of our friends are so busy that we only meet weekly or monthly. But God is always available, so I make it a priority to meet with Him daily. I also set aside a regular time and a regular place. By making those decisions in advance, I'm less likely to let other things interfere with this important friendship.

Where can you meet with God? When you first began this book, I suggested that you find a quiet place to read and think, free of most interruptions and fairly private. It's a bonus if you can find a place you enjoy being—your bedroom, a porch, in your car driving to work, along your regular jogging route. (Yes, you can jog and meet with God at the same time!) I hope you've discovered your place.

When is a good time to meet? Any time that you can stick to. The key lies not in when you meet, but that you schedule time to be with God and you protect your schedule. If you let it just happen, it won't.

Another way to nurture your friendship with God is to **invite variety.** You and your friends don't do exactly the same thing at exactly the same place every time you meet, do you? You may have book group friends, but you also meet sometimes for lunch or to take a garden tour. You may have tennis friends whom you also like to shop with. Yet when we meet with God, we get the idea that we must follow a rigid structure that never varies. Not so!

When I was a young mom, my "quiet time" with God sometimes consisted of sticking printed verse cards on the diaper table and refrigerator where I could see them numerous times a day. I'd pray as I rocked one of the boys or while I showered. Once the boys entered school and car pools became a regular feature of my life, I'd keep an extra Bible in my car with some writing paper. Then I could read, write, and pray while waiting in line. Now I like to run with God in the morning. It's a twist on the old hymn: "And He walks with me and He talks with me." Well, God runs with me!

Friendships also thrive when we **allow time simply to talk.** This has been a benefit of running with God, though your time to talk with God might be while preparing dinner or riding the subway to work or folding the laundry—or all of the above. When I talk with God on my runs, I share whatever is on my mind—what I'm happy about, what confuses me, what I think I need, what I'm trying to make sense of. I ask God lots of questions—He can handle it! I'm as real with God as I know how to be. That's the way it should be between friends.

Finally, just as with any other friendship, a friendship with God thrives when we **take time to listen.** I want to know what God thinks. Midway through most of my jogs, my mind-set shifts from talking to God to listening to God. Listening is a wise thing to do: "If any of you lacks wisdom, you should ask God, who gives generously" (James 1:5 NIV). If I hear from God during my jog, I quickly write down what He impressed upon me once I get home.

All of these activities and habits I've described focus on one essential thing: a relationship. Hearing God flows from knowing

God. Knowing God flows from being with Him. The more time we spend with Him, the easier it becomes to recognize when a nudge or idea or impression is from God. Our ears become tuned to the sound of His voice. We know it's God speaking because, well, it just sounds like the God we've come to know.

Until that deep relationship develops, I suggest you go about discerning God's voice the way your physician goes about diagnosing your needs. I've noticed that my doctor begins by ruling things out, and that's a good way to start with discerning God's voice. We can avoid a lot of confusion by taking into account what God would *not* say to us. For example:

- God will never condemn us (Romans 8:1). If I am hearing things like "Shame on you!" or "Look what a mess you've made," then I know it is not God speaking.
- God will never tempt us (James 1:13).
- God will never lead us to do something in opposition to the teachings of the Bible.

Henry Blackaby's book *Experiencing God* details three ways God most often communicates with us:

- God can use His Word to speak to us.
- God can use His people to speak to us.
- God can use circumstances to speak to us.

If you would like to explore this topic more deeply, I recommend you read Blackaby's excellent insights.

Back to the Dash

Let's return to the dash we talked about earlier, that bit of punctuation that represents all that happens between your first breath and your last. And let's make it personal. You know the date to the left of the dash: it's your birth date. But imagine that the date to the *right* of the dash occurs one week from now. With time running out, would you be willing to do whatever God asked you to do to receive all God has waiting for you?

If you keep my commands, you will remain in my love . . . I have told you this so that my joy may be in you and that your joy may be complete. My command is this: Love each other as I have loved you. (Jesus in John 15:10–12 NIV)

Complete joy—that's what Jesus promises to those who obey Him. And one reason for that joy is this: once you step on the path He has shown you, He will walk it with you. This is not a God who asks the impossible of you and then waits for you to fail. No way! This is the God that Paul described in Philippians 1:6: "Being confident of this, that he who began a good work in you will carry it on to completion" (NIV).

You stand at the crossroads of a life so much "immeasurably more" than you can even "ask or imagine" (Ephesians 3:20 NIV). Whatever burdens you carry—whatever wounds, failures, mistakes, sins—you may be on the verge of becoming God's greatest miracle. Will you believe His promises? Will you seize His timing?

MAKE IT YOURS
Timing Is Everything

1. Psalm 90:10 describes our lives as lasting 70, maybe 80, years. Let's do a little math. Let's say we'll live 75 years. If we multiply 75 years times 365 days per year, we come up with 27,000 days (rounded off). Now multiply your age times 365. Subtract that amount from 27,000. How many days remain?

2. Read Psalm 39:5, Psalm 144:4, and James 4:14. Combined with the math exercise you just did, how do these verses affect your perspective about the years ahead of you?

3. What does Psalm 90:12 teach us about how to respond to the brevity of life?

4. At the beginning of the chapter, we read Ecclesiastes 3:1–8. Circle the events that the writer of Ecclesiastes identified as shaping our lives.

5. Some of those events imply great joy; others suggest sadness and regret. What encouragement does verse 11 give about the events of our lives?

6. You've read how I've perceived God's perfect timing in my life. Describe a time when you experienced God's perfect timing (financial relief, an encouraging phone call, etc.).

7. Are you more naturally inclined to over-wait for God and postpone obedience or to under-wait God and rush into things?

8. In this chapter, we discovered that a well-nurtured relationship with Christ is key to discerning God's timing. What are four ways we can go deeper with that relationship?

9. What is one step you want to take to deepen your friendship with God?

10. In transforming your burdens to blessings so far, you have done one of the hardest parts—taking time for yourself. By stopping life's busyness to look courageously into your mirror and acknowledge your bagged burden, you faced what you had safely tucked away yet could not forget. You have taken a step toward believing that God can do all that He has promised. Last week you isolated the lies that hurt has brought into your life, and you looked at scriptural truths to replace the hurt of the lies with the hope and healing power of God's promise that He is able to work within you and your burden to do abundantly more than you could dare to ask or even imagine (Ephesians 3:20).

Second Corinthians 6:2 says, "Now is the time" (NIV). Today is the day to seize God's timing and continue that reversal from burden to blessing. If you are ready, complete the following sentence:

Now, on today's date of _____, I sense God encouraging me not to harden my heart as I have done in the past by _____

_____, but rather to seize His timing by acknowledging that now is the time to _____

_____. I choose to let Him work through me, providing the faith and strength I need so He may accomplish His transformation of my burden into a blessing.

Journal Notes

CHAPTER FOUR

Fight for Your Future

For the eyes of the Lord range throughout the earth
to strengthen those whose hearts are fully committed to him.
—2 Chronicles 16:9 (NIV)

R emember the leukemia phone call I told you about in chapter one? After Mother's death I had returned to my "normal" life—leading a women's ministry, singing in the choir, similar activities that allowed me to hide behind a mask of respectability. The activities were worthy; my pretense was not.

The phone call about my "probable diagnosis" stopped me in my spiritual tracks. I was acutely aware of what such news could imply. As you now know, I walked across my kitchen, through the family room, and began making my way up the stairs until the weight of it all—the phone call, Mother's death, my sham of a life—came crashing down. I made it as far as the seventh step and was unable to go further. That's where Jesus made His way to meet with me.

He didn't come as you might expect; there was little fanfare and precious few warm and fuzzy moments. Similar to His fateful encounter with the Samaritan woman, Jesus came with truth about me and my life.

The Unmasking

Sitting on that step, I realized I had lost all sense of my authentic self since being dragged from the loving arms of my grandparents. In its place I had learned the protective benefits of conforming and pleasing. Surrendering my self-worth to the definitions of others, being the "right" size, producing the best grades, earning the Miss Teen Time title—these were avenues of acceptance I had pursued through the teen years. As an adult, my badges of significance were Estee Lauder, designer jeans, and staying busy with philanthropic endeavors. I'm not disparaging any of these achievements; it was my motivation in seeking them that I ridicule. Their chief purpose was to mask a wounded heart.

If the heart-wrenching crisis of being taken from my beloved grandparents had been the initiation into a life of wearing masks, I now sensed that this leukemia scare was about to yank me out of my lifestyle of pretense. And I was pretty sure the process would not be easy.

But beneath the cloud of fear that hung over my head, wisdom whispered in my ear: *Jesus doesn't say pretense or perfectionism will set you free. He says truth will unlock the hurts of your heart and the door to freedom!*

My Place of Truth

Just as Jesus once made His way to the crossroads of Jacob's Well to meet the Samaritan woman, I have no doubt He had made His way to Evans, Georgia, to meet with me as well. While not a flesh and blood encounter, I knew I was in His presence that day. But that wasn't totally reassuring. For with my vile version of "truth" flashing before me, I was consumed by a devastating sadness and disappointment with my life, and I was sure Jesus felt the same way when He looked at me. I had secretly condemned myself for so long that I expected the same from Him.

Like the Samaritan woman, I kept trying to divert the conversation to other things, and even to blame other people. But Jesus kept bringing the dialogue back to me. He didn't come dismissing my sin, my abuse, my anger, my masking. He came with something much better: a way in which to use them. Condemnation had come from living half-truths; He was offering to complete my life with His truth. I just wasn't sure how He could do it.

This Man Named Jesus

I wasn't the first not to understand what Jesus had come to do. From time to time, those who knew Him best, the disciples, had a hard time understanding Him as well. His ways seemed too simplistic. His ways were not comparable to the religious laws of that day. Where were all the rules, the to-do lists? Jesus did what others did not allow themselves to do: He reached across social and ethnic boundaries to touch all who needed Him—the outcast and the wealthy tax collector alike, even a Samaritan woman!

As Jesus ministered in His unorthodox way, He recognized the concern and discouragement on His disciples' faces. "Do not let your hearts be troubled," He told them. Thomas identified his struggle to understand Jesus when he asked, "Lord, we don't know where you are going, so how can we know the way?" Jesus answered, "I am the way and the truth and the life" (John 14:1, 5–6 NIV).

As I sat on the step, I was wondering the same thing as Thomas. *Where are You going, Jesus, with all this garbage You are dredging up?* (Did He not understand I had spent a lifetime hiding this mess of heartbreak, shame, and regret?) *Now that You've dug it up, what do You want me to do with it? How do I even begin?*

Where I was going, I found out, was not as important as who I was going with. "Do not let your hearts be troubled" was Jesus' way of saying, "Trust Me, Kim. Will you just trust Me?" But that was asking a lot of someone whose trust had been shattered at the tender age of four.

Unbeknown to me, Jesus was returning me to my starting place. After I had spent a lifetime trying to escape that place, He was taking my hand and walking me back to where it had all begun. He had to show me that even there, in my greatest hurt, He could love and complete me.

Battles of My Mind

If you could have seen the "word battle" going on in my mind it would have looked like a jumbled mess. "You're not OK!" "You're a mistake!" "You can be OK." "What does it matter?" "Jesus loves you." Confusion, devastation, hope, lies, truth: they all fought for my attention. And each time I contemplated God's invitation to work in my life, the mind battle would escalate.

As I floundered amid all the sad truths I had stuffed within my life, I realized I was drowning in what were only half-truths. Jesus had previously shown me the truth about my life but then added His hope to my truth: "You are not OK, but you can be!" I wanted to be OK, but with all that He had made me revisit, I was struggling to believe a transformation was possible.

Have you ever witnessed anyone drowning? That day I felt like I was drowning—without water! The thing is, drowning victims rarely recognize the treacherous depths of the water into which they've floundered or how isolated they have become—until they realize that they are in real trouble. I lived with the loneliness of isolation, and I knew I was in over my head the moment I began to climb those stairs at Brandermill Road. What I didn't know was how much fight I had in me. Saving drowning victims is very difficult because they struggle so fiercely as soon as panic sets in. They know they need help to survive, yet they fend off anyone who comes to save them.

Well, a similar panic had set in for me that day. I knew I needed to be rescued, but I was fighting against my Rescuer with every excuse I had.

Are you relating to this? Maybe by now you're drowning in emotions and feeling a bit panicked too. The daily struggles you face can be just as intense as the battle for life waged by a drowning victim. You don't think so? Look at your bed linens after a restless and sleepless night of worry. Those twisted and disarranged sheets and blankets tell a story.

Of course, our struggle is not with water. The Bible tells us, "Our struggle is not against flesh and blood, but against the rulers, against the authorities, against the powers of this dark world and against the spiritual forces of evil" (Ephesians 6:12 NIV). A battle was raging, and I was being called upon to fight like I'd never fought before.

Two Plans for Every Life

Have you been told, "God has a plan for your life"? It's true. Jeremiah 29:11 says, "'For I know the plans I have for you,' declares the Lord, 'plans to prosper you and not to harm you, plans to give you hope and a future'" (NIV).

That plan is so precise that even good works have been planned with you in mind: "For we are God's handiwork, created in Christ Jesus to do good works, which God prepared in advance for us to do" (Ephesians 2:10 NIV).

Pretty incredible, don't you think? But there is another plan at work for you as well, one you may not have been told about. "Your enemy the devil prowls around like a roaring lion looking for someone" (1 Peter 5:8 NIV).

Someone, anyone, you, me? And why? What is the enemy's plan for you and me? "To steal and kill and destroy" according to John 10:10 (NIV). "To devour" according to 1 Peter 5:8

(NIV). Just as God comes with His plan of an abundant life, the enemy comes to dismiss your purpose, interrupt your plan, and ultimately destroy your life as God has planned it. The result: a life-and-death battle.

How does the enemy execute his battle plans? He begins with your thoughts. The enemy launches his attack by distorting your thinking. First, he makes you doubt that what God has said can ever happen—or that it might happen for some people but not for you—and then he continually discourages you with feelings of inadequacy or uselessness. If you persist in believing God can change your burdens into blessings, the enemy strives to convince you that it is too late to change.

I am sorry to say that his plan of attack against me worked for years and years. I believed his lies. My mind was bursting with the enemy's ridicule and distortions that I had accepted as truth.

Pick the Right Battle

Another tactic of the enemy is to get us to fight the wrong battles. I had spent my life battling to refute the circumstances of my life. But that battle only dragged me down into despair and deception and multiplied the masks I hid behind.

Yes, my life was not the fairy tale the princess-child had dreamed it would be. Yes, I had messed up and let the pain lead me into anorexia, diet pills, anger. Yes, I had fallen short. Yes, I wished I had done some things differently. Yes, I was victimized. No, life had not turned out the way I thought it was "supposed" to. I could go on and on. But I needed to quit fighting that battle, and so do you. Whatever happened has happened. As repulsive or regrettable as you may find your past, as unfair as it may seem, as deeply as you hurt, no amount of wrestling can change what has already occurred. *The fight is to change your future.*

Did you hear that? Stop fighting your past and the One who

has come to rescue you, and fight for your future! You have already begun by acknowledging the truth about yourself; now let's give Jesus freedom to complete you with His truth.

Stop fighting your past, and fight for your future.

Wanted: Imperfect People

Let me ask you something: What is the yardstick against which you measure yourself? Is it the yardstick of God's truth? Or is it the perceptions you've formed based on others' superficial and worldly judgments about what is right and what is wrong? Is it the billboard signs or the magazine covers? Or may I carefully wade in and ask: Is it the standard you perceive among those active little church people (a group of which I am a member)? Do they all appear to be happy, perfect Christians?

Oh come on! Who among us will be the first to confess we are not perfect? Who will be first to reject the limits that lie has placed on us?

There are many examples of biblical heroes who could have felt unworthy and very limited because of things in their past. Consider the following scriptural examples of God using decidedly imperfect lives. On their own merits, none of these people enjoyed a desirable place of truth. That came only as they allowed God to complete their lives with His truth. But I want you to look at what they would have missed had they lived only within their own truth.

- Joseph's place of truth—a bragging, spoiled-brat-turned-slave and ex-con—did not limit him from saving his family (the twelve tribes of Israel and the ancestors of Christ).

- Rahab's place of truth—a prostitute—did not limit her from playing a pivotal role in helping the Israelites take the Promised Land.
- Esther's place of truth—a slave girl married to a Gentile—did not prevent her from saving God's people from an impending massacre.
- Mary's place of truth—an unmarried peasant girl—did not prevent her from being chosen to be the mother of Jesus.
- Peter's place of truth—a hotheaded, egotistical fisherman—did not prevent him from becoming the leader of the first church and author of two New Testament letters.

Somewhere along their life journey, these people faced the truth that they were not OK. And the enemy stepped in with the lie that they were too imperfect, too "not OK" for God to use. But the evidence of their lives tells us that each one of them rejected the lie and instead embraced the truth of the message God gave me: "But you can be!"

The Journey to "You Can Be"

Like almost everything that really matters in life, the path toward what we can be in Christ is a process. Here are the key markers along that path.

"You Can Be" by Facing Your Truth. What battles rage in your mind today? Sitting in this Bible study or in the quietness of your home, where has each chapter, each truth, each Scripture reference taken you? What words echo in your mind and heart today, and which clash violently with the lies you've ordered your life around?

Like me, you may not be proud of where your hurts have taken you. I think you see from my story that I truly understand. You may not want to face that addiction, or move past the hurt, or quit making excuses for your abuser. I don't know what burdens you bear, but *you* do—and more importantly, Jesus does. I have to take you back again to Psalm 51:6: "You desire truth in the inward parts" (NKJV). To move ahead, I had to be honest with myself at each interval along the way, and so must you. You may think it is rather presumptuous of me to believe that you want to move ahead. But don't you? I can't imagine anyone sitting through this self-examining, gut-wrenching study who was completely content with her status quo. You want more!

> Sad is the day for any man when he becomes absolutely satisfied with the life that he is living, the thoughts he is thinking and the deeds he is doing; until there ceases to be forever beating at the door of his soul a desire to do something larger which he seeks and knows he was meant and intended to do.*

Can you identify with Phillips Brooks' words? Do you recognize yourself as someone who is not "absolutely satisfied with the life [you are] living"? You have decided not to settle for less than God's best, all that you know you were "meant and intended to do." Your heart for God and His promises has been reawakened: You are ready to fight for your future. Your time is now! Let Jesus take you back to all those hurts and places from which you have been running. Confront your truth so Jesus can complete you with His.

Remember the battle of my mind that I described a few pages ago—the words and phrases that represented the lies I had allowed to shape me and the truths I longed to believe? What words represent your battle? At the top of a sheet of paper, put "(Your Name's)

---

* Phillips Brooks, as cited by John C. Maxwell, *Be All You Can Be* (Colorado Springs, CO: David C. Cook, 2007), 32.

Battle for the Mind." Then make a list like I did. Don't worry that it isn't nice and pretty. God isn't bothered by that. He wants you to face what you believe to be true. Then we'll face together what God says is really true.

Before an exercise like this, I find it helpful to ask God for His perspective. Here's a sample prayer that may help you.

Dear Father,

It's me! The real me. I come with my bag—that brown paper bag that's been tucked deep inside my heart. For years, this brown bag is the place I have stowed every part of me that I haven't known what to do with—whatever seemed sad or repulsive or worthless, whatever I feared might make others think less of me. For so long I thought I'd safely hidden away all those ugly, hurtful bits and pieces. I thought they were powerless. Now I'm beginning to understand that it is actually the hurts inside my brown paper bag that have influenced my thinking and my actions for many years. How many areas of my life have they affected? Are they why I cry at certain things or become so uncontrollably outraged at others? Have they altered my personality? Has my spiritual life suffered because these were the parts of me that always shouted that I don't measure up? Has it been the contents of that ugly brown paper bag that have whispered words of unworthiness in my heart for so long? Are they the reason for my feelings of insignificance whenever I walk into a room full of people? Dear Father, I believe You have made Your way to this place to meet me today. Give me eyes to see You and ears to hear You. You say, "Come to Me," so here I am, just as I am. Please help me open this brown paper bag and continue with my truth. Amen.

Now, be still. Listen. What are you hearing? Add it to your list. As difficult as this exercise may be, you have just taken a huge step toward what "You Can Be."

"You Can Be" by Understanding Why You, Why Now. I was so embarrassed. Had I only been alerted to the fact Jesus was coming to Brandermill Road, I would have been better prepared. I would have had more Scripture memorized. I would have prayed harder and longer. But He hadn't called ahead, had given no preparation time. *Why me? Why now?* I wondered.

Are you wondering the same thing? Why, you ask, were you drawn to this study after all these years? I have a feeling it has to do with the urgency of your future. Perhaps after the previous chapter, you were motivated, began to move toward change with all kinds of good intentions, and then were sidetracked or sidelined. God understands you well enough to know that you have purposed in your heart to do what He is calling you to do . . . one day. What if "one day" is now? I believe He is so eager to show you the good things He has for you that He can't wait another day. Your "one day" has arrived! Your "one day" is today.

We have established that a set of enemy eyes prowls the earth looking for someone to "steal and kill and destroy" (John 10:10 NIV). That is truth. But here is the total truth: there is another set of eyes looking, seeking. "For the eyes of the Lord range throughout the earth" (2 Chronicles 16:9 NIV).

Very simply, Jesus is always looking for those whose hearts are ready to join Him in His work. Those who are finally ready to turn away from every lie and deception that they have believed. Those ready for the words that encourage, as well as the words that will convict and challenge. Those ready to stretch. Ready to be. Ready to do. How awesome is that! He is looking for those who are ready to commit to Him, those in whose hearts lies a yearning, a "want to." And He has noticed you!

Listen carefully: All those repulsive, hurtful bits of you that shout condescending little messages—they don't intimidate Jesus. All the mistakes, sins, hurts, abuses, abandoned dreams— He wades right on through, proclaiming, "I can work with that!" What you or others may deem spiritually catastrophic, Jesus stands ready and able to put to use. Galatians 2:6 declares, "God isn't impressed with mere appearances" (MSG). All my pretense—it wasn't fooling Him. All my memorized Scripture, all my checkmarks for Sunday school attendance, all my compiled sins and delay tactics do not surprise God. And neither do yours. We may appear polished, strong, together—but He knows us, the real you and me. Thank God! "The Lord does not look at the things people look at. People look at the outward appearance, but the Lord looks at the heart" (1 Samuel 16:7 NIV).

> *All those repulsive, hurtful bits of you that shout condescending messages— they don't intimidate Jesus.*

God knows that when the burdens I carry are set aside and the masks removed, my deepest heart's desire is to be everything He wants me to be and to join Him in completing His work. It is a lie to think I was too messed up or it was too late to be a part of His plan for me.

It gives me great joy to tell you, my friend, that today your heart has caught God's eye too! Why you? Because He "gets" you. He understands you. He knows you through and through, and He loves you. He is bigger than your condemned heart. He finds you worthy. While you and others may only see the externals of what is, God sees the inside and all you can be.

"You Can Be" by Being Strengthened. The "truths" we've

been believing about ourselves not only leave us ashamed, they weaken us. I have a whimsical towel hanging in my kitchen that reads, "It's exhausting being this perfect!" While intended to be lighthearted, that quip accurately describes the heaviness and weakness I felt from years of striving for perfection and juggling a wardrobe of masks so no one would know how far short of perfection I was. But Paul exclaimed, "I delight in weaknesses, in insults, in hardships, in persecutions, in difficulties. For when I am weak, then I am strong."   Where did Paul find his strength? He found in it Christ's power. He realized that only by acknowledging and accepting his weaknesses could he become a recipient of Christ's power—the only power that has the truth to complete our lives no matter how weak we may be today! No wonder Paul also wrote, "When you have Christ, you are complete" (Colossians 2:10 NLV).

Earlier I stated that we are walking around with half-empty lives because we are living with half-filled truths. God stands ready to remedy that for us right now. He can replace our weak half-truths with His strong, unshakeable, eternal truth.

Below are some examples of my incomplete "truths" that I allowed God to complete with His truth.

- My truth is that my foundation was shattered at age four. And once I wasn't OK, but now I am because God's truth has provided me with a solid foundation that stands firm (2 Timothy 2:19).
- My truth is that I suffered shame and abuse. And once I wasn't OK, but I am now because God's truth has brought purpose to my life and double gain for my pain (Isaiah 61:7).
- My truth is that I have made horrible mistakes and sinned. And once I wasn't OK, but I am now because

of God's truth that says when I confessed that sin, Jesus forgave me (1 John 1:9).

- My truth is that I lost my mother. And once I wasn't OK, but today I am because God's truth says I will see her as we spend eternity together in heaven (1 Thessalonians 3:13–18).
- My truth is that I have wasted a lot of time. And once I wasn't OK, but today I am because of God's truth that, at a moment's notice, He can make all things—even those that seem wasted, hurtful, regrettable, or evil—work for my good and His glory (Romans 8:28).

I invite you to try a similar exercise from your life. Identify those words and phrases you battle, identify the lie behind those words, and then identify God's truth. As you progress through this study, you'll probably want to add more truth statements to your list.

"You Can Be" by Being Purposed. What a transformation we saw in the Samaritan woman! From one always in hiding to one running through the streets proclaiming, "Come meet a Man who told me everything I ever did!" She was proclaiming her truth, which had brought her so much pain, but now she was adding God's truth to her story. God had gone beyond others' characterizations of her unfortunate circumstances or bad choices or unworthiness. Jesus had sought her out, made His way to her, seen straight into her heart, and let her know of His love for her—just as she was. He transformed what once had looked like nothing but waste and misery into her unique and personal message. And will you look at what happened: "Many of the Samaritans from that town believed in him because of the woman's testimony" (John 4:39 NIV). Awesome! Awesome! Awesome!

The transformation in Mother's life was no less astonishing, notwithstanding the fact that hers arrived in a very different way from the Samaritan woman's transformation. You see, unlike the Samaritan woman, Mother had always proclaimed God's truths. But she had never been ready to reveal *her* truth. As she lay dying, her honesty, transparency, and vulnerability was all that was needed to free God to work in her life. Her words penetrated my heart, forever changing me and ultimately birthing a national ministry for the One before whom she expected to feel shame. How delighted God must have been at her choice at her last crossroad: to reach beyond all the lies, resisting the temptation to hide, refusing to accept hopelessness, and instead, finally, trusting Him and His promises.

Personal, Practical, Powerful

If you are tired of the status quo of living by lies and ready for God's transforming truth, the biblical principles in this chapter will help you begin to reclaim parts of your life that you thought were forever lost or stolen. By choosing these truths, you can move beyond the mind battles and the lies to what God has waiting for you.

Romans 12:2 exhorts us, "Do not conform to the pattern of this world, but be transformed by the renewing of your mind" (NIV). The minds of believers conform to the pattern of this world in at least two ways:

(1) We live with our truth but fail to complete it with God's truth. When this happens, we walk around knowing something is missing. We know there has to be something more. Some may describe it as emptiness, an unfilled hole in the heart, or a restlessness of the soul. We try the world's offerings—material belongings, titles, status—thinking they'll make us feel complete. But no matter how much we amass, we never feel completed. Instead, we end

up with debt, food addictions, alcoholism, worry, and feelings of inferiority, discouragement, and depression. Or . . .

(2) We live professing God's truths but never acknowledging ours. This is what Mother and I did. We could recite biblical principles, but we weren't willing to acknowledge the truth about ourselves. It was far more important to us to masquerade a near-perfect life than to admit the burdens we carried. Yet daily, yearly, we were paying the price, for without being honest about our pain, we couldn't become what God wanted us to become.

> *Many of us never get to where we want to go because we are not willing to admit where we really are.*

I can't help but think of the GPS in our car. To get to my desired destination, I have to put that address into the system, and then I must enter my starting point. Wouldn't it be foolish to put in an address at the midpoint of my trip, just to cut down on the distance? Silly as it may seem, that is what Mother and I were doing, and I know we are not alone. How many of us never get to where we want to go because we are not willing to admit where we really are?

I have seen this again and again as I travel and speak. We don't like where we are so we just assume a pose and pretend to be something we are not. The sad, sad truth is that we have a clear destination: we want to be all that God has created us to be and to fulfill our unique plan, but we fail to recognize the way to do that—namely, honesty with God, ourselves, and others.

At the beginning of this chapter we talked about the fight we are called to fight—a fight of faith that says no matter the burden, no matter the hurt, I am still *me* and I am reclaiming my life! It's a fight that says, "Right now—even if my life is a mess—I am believing and ready to do whatever God asks so that my life will be just as God has said it will be—not merely marked by externals, but rather a life overflowing with purpose and contentment, one that is abundantly more than anything I can ask or imagine (see Acts 27:25, Ephesians 3:20). God not only sees us as we are presently but also as we are potentially!

Ready to Choose

Sitting on that step, I also had to choose. I was terrified. I didn't have a clue what was about to be asked of me, but I knew I had tried most everything the world had to offer, and it had never been enough to complete me or make me feel that I measured up.

But was what Jesus offered enough? Was it really better than what I had, or is this as good as it gets? I wasn't sure. But I was sure that He had made His way to me on that seventh step, and so I made the choice to take His hand, hoping He could lead me to a better place.

I wasn't sure if it was possible. But I was sure ready to find out. What about you? Are you ready?

MAKE IT YOURS
Fighting for Your Truth

1. In your childhood, with whom did you fight the most? Perhaps a parent—if so, which one? Or were you always at odds with one sibling? Are you still fighting with the same people, or do you fight with someone different today, like your spouse?

2. In this week's chapter, we were reminded that God has a plan for us, but we also discovered that there's another plan. What is that plan?

3. These conflicting plans create a battle in our lives. According to Ephesians 6:12, against whom are we fighting?

4. The fight for our future is not on a visible battlefield. Rather, the battlefield is in our minds. I described my mental battle: the clashing words and phrases of truth and lies that fought against one another. If you haven't already done so, complete for yourself a "Battle of the Mind" exercise described on pages 91–92. List the words and phrases that you have allowed to fill your mind and create your burdens. Write whatever pops into your mind; you will have time to ponder what you wrote later.

5. Our starting place in our battle of the mind is our place of truth. That truth can be a hurtful and painful place where we see our imperfections and may have to acknowledge that we are not OK. But we aren't the only ones who aren't OK! Name

one person from this week's study of imperfect people who brought you hope. What is it about that person that encourages you?

6. What would that person have missed if he or she had given up and not fought for the future?

7. Imperfect people become OK as we allow God to complete our truth with His truth. Let's see how your life, completed and filled with God's truths, can begin to change your mindset today. Create your own "My Truths, God's Truths" exercise like the one I described on pages 95–96. Divide a sheet of paper in half vertically. List some of the half-truths and lies that your burden has used to hurt and condemn you. (Remember, your word battle exercise can help you here.) Then, using some of the Scriptures and principles you've gleaned so far in this book, write a corresponding truth in the right column that reflects God's perspective on your burden. You may not have an exact verse and reference for each of God's truths; that's fine. If you're studying this book in a group, ask someone to help you. In time, you will be able to add verses to your list and even expand your list with new truths you discover. Be prayerful, asking God to reveal important truths and lies about your burden that you may be overlooking.

8. Pull out your brown paper bag with its burden. Think of ways your burden has convinced you that you are not OK. Now think of the truths of God's words and what they promise you. I have heard it said that where the mind goes, the man (or woman!) follows. Are you ready to let God's words lead you from a world of hurt and burdens to your place of blessing? You can take a first step toward committing to fight for your promised blessings by completing this statement:

My truth is that I have tucked in my bag the burden of
_____ and it has robbed me
of how God wants to bless me by making me believe that I
am not OK because _____
_____. But I am realizing that this is only half
the truth of my life, and I am not settling for that any longer. The complete truth is that while I can't go back and
start over, I can start today to fight for a new ending. I can
do this by allowing God to complete my life and make me
OK with His truth that _____

_____.

Journal Notes

CHAPTER FIVE

Step Out and Discover

S tep back into my past with me for a moment. My husband, Lee, and I were returning home after my mother's funeral service. I was filled with more hurt than I thought my heart could endure. The violent thunder and lightning outside our car fit the turmoil within me. Finally, out of view of all the attendees, I gave way to tears of sadness, of anger, of a myriad of emotions.

Lee's voice broke through my wall of emotion. "Kim, open your eyes! You are not going to believe this!" His enthusiasm for whatever it was sickened me. I did not want anyone to interrupt my grieving. Yet he persisted. "Kim, please, just for minute—please, look up!"

Relenting, I opened my eyes. What I saw took my breath away. The darkened skies had given way to light. The thunder had silenced, the lightning halted. And there before me, stretching across the horizon, was the most beautiful rainbow I had ever seen.

I could not help but compare it to another famous rainbow and I wondered: *Is God trying to tell me something?*

Another Rainbow, Another Covenant

In a world "corrupt in God's sight and . . . full of violence," Noah was a righteous man, "blameless among the people . . . he walked faithfully with God." Because Noah had found favor in His eyes, God told Noah of His plan to flood the earth. Every creature would perish, Noah learned, but God promised "I will establish my covenant with you" (Genesis 6:9, 11, 18 NIV).

Do you remember what happened next? God directed Noah to build an ark. How perfectly reasonable! Nothing like building a huge boat before the first raindrop had ever fallen from the sky! Next, God commanded Noah to gather onto this boat his family *plus* two of every animal and living creature. I cannot imagine the thoughts going through Noah's head by this point! And here's the amazing part: "Noah did everything just as God commanded him" (Genesis 6:22 NIV).

Astonishing, don't you think? Especially when you consider it took Noah 120 years to complete the ark. Imagine all he and his family had to endure: ridicule and taunting to be sure, and probably some financial hardship. And they endured these hardships longer than you or I will probably live!

Still, Noah accomplished the mission God gave him. And in return, God gave Noah a promise:

> I now establish my covenant with you and with your descendants after you. . . . Never again will all life be destroyed by the waters of a flood; never again will there be a flood to destroy the earth. . . . I have set my rainbow in the clouds, and it will be the sign of the covenant between me and the earth. (Genesis 9:9–13 NIV)

This is a particular kind of promise called a covenant. A covenant is similar to a contract, but not in the way we think of contracts today. God's covenants are not bilateral. And they're nonnegotiable. God alone initiates, He pledges His faithfulness, He sets the standards. Fulfillment comes only through our obedience to those standards. God had come to Noah with the covenant, Noah determined to obey all the commandments in the covenant, and he completed all that was required of him, thereby receiving God's blessings.

The story of Noah and that first rainbow was very familiar to me on the day of Mother's funeral, when Lee pointed out a new rainbow to me, so you can see why I suspected that God had a message for me.

Yes, I was hurting. No, events had not unfolded as I had so desperately prayed.

Yes, God could have prevented Mother's death from cancer; but no, He had not. Yes, I was questioning, doubting, trying to make sense of it all. But no, I simply could not understand. That was my truth.

This rainbow, however, was another way of God making His way to me and bringing *His* truth to me. It pointed me to my Bible where, in the weeks that followed, I read God's promises. Some of those promises leaped from the pages as if written just for me, and ultimately I summarized them in a sort of personal declaration of confidence in what God intended for my life. Imagine my delight when I realized that my promise summary matched the acronym "Roy G. Biv," the memory tool I was taught as a child for recalling the seven colors of the rainbow: red, orange, yellow, green, blue, indigo, and violet.

If you **R**emember
And choose to **O**bey,
Then no matter **Y**our circumstances,
God is **B**igger!
He takes burdens in your life that seem **I**mpossible today
And transforms them into **V**ictorious blessings for tomorrow!

Let's look in more detail at the rainbow of promises God gave me during that period.

If you Remember . . .

Before I formed you in the womb I knew you.
I set you apart and appointed you!
You were labeled "Made in Heaven"
and stamped "Very Good."
I have declared a plan, a purpose, just for you.
This purpose is composed of many good works
that were planned in advance for you to do.

And choose to Obey . . .

If you listen, I will tell you the plan.
You can know my voice as I whisper,
"This is the way, walk in it."

Then no matter Your circumstances . . .

Certain things I tell you in advance as a warning!
You will have trials and tribulations.
You will suffer disappointments and losses.
And you will not always understand.

God (God. Period. Nothing else. He is all you need.) . . .

But through it all you will never be alone,
even in the darkest of times.
I will be there!
So you will know that I, the Lord,
I, who created the heavens and stretched them out,
who spread forth the earth and that which comes from it,
who gives breath to the people on it,
It is I, the Lord, who loves you so much
that I gave my only begotten Son, Jesus,
that if you believe in Him,
you will never perish
but will begin an eternal life.

*Is **Bigger** than anything from your past or anything in your future . . .*
It is I, the Lord, for whom nothing in your life is impossible!
I see you. I know your hurts.
I will always be near when you have a broken heart.
You can cry out to me and I will answer.
And when you fall down, I will pick you up with My hand.
And when people hurt you, when they intend evil . . .

*He takes burdens in your life that seem **Impossible** today . . .*
Just wait upon Me. I will turn it to good!
With whatever happens in your life, you can trust Me.
And when you can't understand, follow Me anyway!
I am always working, whether you see it or not!
Anything you may regret,
those things you have endured or suffered,
the hurts of your heart,
have become the richness of who you are.
And from the darkness of those hurts,
even those secrets you have hidden,
and the burdens that you bear,
I stand right in the middle of them,
ready and able to make them work for good
by gifting them with purpose,
while continuing the plan I have declared for you.

*And transforms them into **Victorious** blessings for tomorrow!*
In all that you are and all you have experienced,
you have become uniquely equipped to reach others who hurt.
By reaching them, you will be blessed
while becoming a blessing.
And you'll discover right now,
today,
that at any time you can begin a life

exceeding abundantly above anything
you ever asked, thought, or even dared to imagine!

(Based on the promises of Jeremiah 1:5; Psalm 139:13; Jeremiah 29:11; Ephesians 2:10; John 10:27; Isaiah 30:21; John 16:33; Hebrews 13:5; Psalm 34:18; Jeremiah 33:3; Psalm 37:24; Genesis 50:20; Proverbs 3:5–7; Isaiah 45:3; Romans 8:28; Luke 1:37; and Ephesians 3:20.)

A Decision Is Made

These are great, great promises with not even a hint of false advertising in them. That's because God has power to do what He has promised (Romans 4:21). I have found this to be true firsthand. And not only does He have the power, but "he who promised is faithful" (Hebrews 10:23 NIV). These are the twin truths I focused on during my time on that seventh step. As I remembered the incredible rainbow on the day of Mother's funeral, and the promises God had given me since then, something clicked within me. I didn't want to resist any longer. I was ready to focus my attention and hang my hope on God's rainbow of promises. I wanted the promised life, not some cheap facsimile. I wanted, as best I could, to align my life to His words by doing whatever God said and seeing what would happen. It was no longer enough for me to believe that God's words were true; I was ready for that truth to affect the way I lived, the choices I made, the thoughts I allowed to govern me, and more.

> *I was ready for God's truth to affect the way I lived, the choices I made, the thoughts I allowed to govern me.*

I found great inspiration in Abraham. Listen to how Paul describes Abraham in the book of Romans:

Against all hope, Abraham in hope believed and so became the father of many nations, just as it had been said to him, "So shall your offspring be." Without weakening in his faith, he faced the fact that his body was as good as dead—since he was about a hundred years old—and that Sarah's womb was also dead. Yet he did not waver through unbelief regarding the promise of God, but was strengthened in his faith and gave glory to God, being fully persuaded that God had power to do what he had promised. (Romans 4:18–21 NIV)

Abraham put all his trust in God even when there seemed to be no hope. He could have been discouraged had he only looked at *his* truth—that he was old and his wife was barren—but he knew he had to believe before he would ever see. I think the key to his great faith is found in verse 17 of that same chapter in Romans. It says his faith was in "the God who gives life to the dead and calls into being things that were not" (NIV).

Abraham believed he would become the father of all nations even when it was physically impossible. Noah believed God when He said a flood was coming—and took action. The Samaritan woman believed her life could be changed and ran back into town with the news of a man named Jesus.

And now I believed. I knew the truth of my life, and the hurdles before me seemed overwhelming. But I also now knew that He "calls into being things there were not" (Romans 4:17 NIV). If God said I could be OK, I was ready to accept it as already accomplished somewhere in my future. My responsibility was to keep walking toward that future, to step beyond my comfort level and my preconceived notions of my abilities or inabilities to discover what God could do through me.

What about you? What seems impossible to you? What seems

dead? Your marriage? Your dreams? What seems too large to conquer? Your depression? An illness? An abuse you have suffered? A habit? Your negative self-talk? Your worries? Your fears?

Are you tired of being stuck? I was! I was tired of feeling defeated, depressed, and damaged, tired of feeling discouraged and hopeless. I knew it would not be easy, but I determined to face my truth head on—and complete my truth with God's truth. "In Him you have been made complete" (Colossians 2:10 NASB). My truth and yours—no matter how accurately we perceive it—is only part of the story. Are you ready to believe that with me and act upon it?

Ready or Not, God, Here I Come!

Having immersed myself in God's promises, I now had new resolve and determination to discover the life He created me to live. But I needed to know more about what pursuing that new life might look like. I looked up the word *pursue* in my Bible's concordance and discovered 1 Timothy 6:11–12. There, Paul instructs Timothy to "pursue righteousness, godliness, faith, love, endurance and gentleness. Fight the good fight of the faith. Take hold of the eternal life to which you were called" (NIV).

Wow! Wow! Wow! These forceful verbs were rather frightening to a confrontation-averse Southern gal. I was all for sitting in a pew and singing stirring hymns. But I was not a fighter. I was no taker.

As my resolve floundered, God reminded me of a familiar person from Scripture who was not unlike me in that moment. Good ol' Peter, the fisherman.

In Matthew 14, we see Peter moving from an earnest desire to demonstrate the extent of his faith in Jesus ("I can walk on water!") to a frightened floundering when his faith failed him ("Yikes! Wind!"). I think Peter became so enamored with his desire to do something great for Jesus that he lost sight of the One he wanted to please. He lost sight of Jesus.

> Then Peter got down out of the boat, walked on the water and came toward Jesus. But when he saw the wind, he was afraid and, beginning to sink, cried out, "Lord, save me!" Immediately Jesus reached out his hand and caught him. (Matthew 14:29–31 NIV)

Can you see why this story spoke so personally to me? It was as if, before I had a chance to sink in my own sea of doubt, God reached out and showed me what to do. These three principles He gave me that day from Peter's life continue to help me stay afloat many years later.

First, I had to get out of the boat, the place I had found comfortable and safe from the storms of life. The place where I could hide and pretend.

Second, I had to go alone. Peter didn't wait to see if all his buddies were coming and neither could I! Was I willing to be the first one to take off my masks? Maybe even the only one?

Third, I needed to keep my eyes on Jesus. Now that He had caught my attention and showed me a different way of life, I would have to stay focused on following only Him no matter how stormy it got outside the boat.

What About You?

Does my story resonate with you at all? Have you known moments when Scripture spoke with an intensely personal voice to your heart? Have you known with striking clarity what Jesus wanted you to do but drawn back out of fear or indifference or confusion?

When I think about how long it took me to come around to following Jesus with all my being, or when I'm filled with remorse for resisting Him, I recall my mother. Only at the end of her life did she realize the futility of anything other than God's way. And as she lay on her deathbed, Jesus issued yet another invitation to join Him, to trust Him completely. Again, she faced and pondered the possibility of God's promises. "I have a plan," He told her. "I can make all things good." Even in the face of death, I believe these words stirred hope in Mother. But she must have also remembered these words: "But I demand truth." Now, added to all the other lies she had listened to during her life were new lies: "It's too late! What difference can it make now? What good could possibly come from your tragedies, your mistakes, your life?" I vividly imagine how these lies warred against the truth Jesus was speaking to her: "I have a plan. I can make all things good. God calls things that are not as though they were."

At her final crossroad, Mother chose a different path. Don't get me wrong: She had walked with God throughout her life and loved Him with all her heart. But she had not always *believed* God, especially when it came to how He wanted to transform her life. Now, however, still without understanding *how* God would work, she chose to believe His promises—the ones she had always doubted—and to act upon her belief. I know it was difficult: recalling the outward signs of her internal battle still brings me to tears. I can still see her chemo-stricken body, her head bowed as if shamed by her disease. But I also saw a resolve in her eyes I had never seen before. And though her voice was weak, her words were powerful.

In a rare moment of truth, transparency, and vulnerability, Mother found Mother! She returned to the woman she had left behind so long ago, buried in hurt, hidden in darkness. At the very moment Mother spoke truth about herself, God was free to continue His work. And part of His work was to use my mother's words of truth as a springboard to my own healing and ultimately as a springboard to the healing of thousands of women with whom I share our story.

God took Mother's truth and her vulnerability and gifted them with purpose to bring meaning and completion to her life. I wonder if He whispered to her, "I will give you treasures from within the darkness and hidden riches from the secret places" (Isaiah 45:3; my paraphrase). For that is surely what He did.

Baby Steps

Jeremiah 6:16 says, "Stand at the crossroads and look . . . Ask where the good way is,and walk in it" (NIV).

Now that I was out of the boat, I took these words literally. Four practical principles emerged from what Jeremiah was saying that helped me make the transition from scriptural print to situational practice. I determined to make this passage a motto in my life. So I stopped my running and my denying and I stood still at my crossroad. Next, I looked around and I confronted my truth. Then, I asked God to show me the "good way." And I began to take baby steps as God gave me directions.

I knew that my first steps toward any change in my life had to begin with authenticity. Simply said, God wanted me to be me. It sounds so effortless, doesn't it? If it were not so sad, it would be laughable. But I had to figure out who "me" really was. My foundation had been shattered when I was an innocent little girl, and I had left the spirit of "me" back in that terrible pain. My journey began by reconnecting with who I was as a child in order to understand who I had become and how my life experiences had shaped me. God, I knew, could intertwine all that into His plan for me— but my role was to look at the truth about myself and not shy away from it. Only in doing so could I become "confident of this very thing, that He who has begun a good work in [me] will complete it" one tiny but courageous step at a time (Philippians 1:6 NKJV).

Proverbs 23:23 gave me a framework for my ongoing pursuit of God: "Get wisdom and instruction and understanding"

(NASB). I realized that all of my contrived busyness was a poor substitute for the kind of discipline that made time for God. I needed to prioritize my days to allow me to spend time with God, to sit at my well and talk with Him. Only in God's presence could I count on receiving the wisdom and understanding I needed to move forward.

> *Only in God's presence could I count on receiving the wisdom and understanding I needed to move forward.*

I know I have written already about the need for devoting time each day to being with God. But because it can be so difficult to slow down and make that time, I want to reiterate its importance and give you a few practical pointers. There are many ways to achieve this quiet time with God, and as you experiment you will find what works best for you. I roll out of bed in the quietness of the morning, read my Bible, jump into some running shoes, and take off. I start my morning jog with a praise song to get focused, and then I simply talk to God. Big things, little things—over the years He has heard it all. But after I have talked it all out, I always conclude my time in silence, listening to His voice. Leviticus 26:12 motivates me: "I will walk with you and be your God" (NCV).

Back home from my walk or jog, I journal what I believe God said to me. Many times, I write down an action step He showed me to take.

This routine might not be your thing at all. You may prefer an overstuffed chair in the den, with a large mug of coffee close at hand and the Bible in your lap. Maybe your best times with God take place late at night when the rest of the household is asleep. The details are up to you; I just urge you to do this one thing—set aside some small chunk of time each day to talk to God and listen to Him. I assure you, He will become real to you as never before. You will experience the truth of Isaiah 30:21: "Whether you turn to the right or to the left, your ears will hear a voice behind you, saying, 'This is the way; walk in it'" (NIV).

My Step Toward Me

So I began my journey toward authenticity by meeting faithfully with God. As I spent time with Him, I discovered that—though I couldn't always see the big picture—as soon as I was obedient in taking a single step, God would reveal the next step He would have me take. My progress was in direct proportion to my obedience.

> *As soon as I was obedient in taking a single step, God would reveal the next step.*

Not long after establishing my habit of spending time with Him, God impressed upon me that I needed to reveal the real me to my husband. "To your husband?" you may ask. "Even *he* didn't know you?" That's right. Not the *real* me. I wasn't exaggerating when I told you how skilled I was at wearing masks, hiding behind walls, and manipulating circumstances and timing. I'd had years of practice! This man had been part of my life for almost six years by then, first as the man I was dating and then as my husband, yet I had never revealed to him my childhood hurts, my anorexia, my constant self-criticism, my insecurities. And so that next step was anything but easy. Still, I was so determined that I did it anyway. I shared all of me with him. Rather than pushing me away, he loved me anyway—perhaps even more.

Lee's support was an enormous gift. With his acceptance and encouragement, I was even more determined to push ahead. That Scripture about fighting the good fight of faith? Even this

Southern gal was learning to fight. Of course, I had to fight the same old voices that echoed in my ears, *You don't want to do this! Big, big, major mistake! You are only going to embarrass yourself!*

But the truth was, I did want to do it—whatever God asked. I did want to believe God's promises about my life and to see their fruition in my life. My resolve led me again and again to God's Word. I read about the faith of others, and it inspired me toward greater obedience. And one day this Scripture practically jumped off the page at me:

> Therefore, since we are surrounded by such a great cloud of witnesses, let us throw off everything that hinders and the sin that so easily entangles, and let us run with perseverance the race marked out for us. (Hebrews 12:1 NIV)

God had already used Peter and Jeremiah to give me practical ways to move forward with Him. Now He was using Paul's words to show me four additional guiding principles. I call these the four Rs for the journey.

Renew. The Bible is replete with stories from that "cloud of witnesses," people whose faith accomplished great things. One reason those stories are there, I believe, is to renew our faith when it falters. We are reminded that we too can become who God created us to be and accomplish what He wants us to do. I was encouraged to know I was on the right track in turning regularly to these stories so my faith could keep growing.

Rid. We're urged to get rid of everything that hinders us and the sins that entangle. Everything? Are you kidding me? Depression, anorexia, masking, deception, fear—I had lots of work to do. But I came to understand that we have to be emptied of that which isn't useful to make room for that which is. It helped to remind myself that, if needed, I could work on ridding myself of one hindrance at a time. Ridding is a process.

Reconcile. I identified this as step three when I asked myself, *What is it that hinders me most?* Time and again, God emphasizes our relationships with one another. Yet lack of forgiveness was my root sin. I had ignored the teaching of Matthew 5:23–24: "If you are offering your gift at the altar and there remember your brother or sister has something against you, leave your gift . . . [and] first go and be reconciled . . . then come and offer your gift" (NIV).

I had seen how reconciliation worked with Mother, but there were others I wasn't sure I could—or even wanted to—forgive! This third step was going to be a big one for me, I could tell.

Run. The final directive in this passage identified my fourth step, and there is an urgency behind the directive. Run! Once you know what to do, do it! Here's an interesting observation: we are to run the race *marked out for us.* That tells me that not everyone has the same race. How could we? Each of us has different experiences, different hurts, different passions, and therefore different ways to find purpose and meaning in our lives. Everyone receives salvation the same way—through Jesus—but we live out that salvation in ways as unique as we are.

Help, I Need Somebody!

I was encouraged by these insights from Hebrews, but I was also overwhelmed. Renew. Rid. Reconcile. Run. (Not to mention Discipline! Prioritize! Focus!) Whew! I didn't know which end was up.

One thing I did know: I absolutely could not do this alone. I needed help. But where would I find help? Who could I trust?

Acutely aware of my need for companions in my journey of belief and obedience, I began to notice women I admired. In each, I saw a particular attribute I wanted in my life. For example, in Bev I saw a quiet strength; in Kaye, a godly confidence; in Dovie, the ease of laughter and great fun; and in Dawn, tremendous commitment. In these women, I saw the woman I wanted to become.

I had no idea at that time, but as I was seeking God's guidance in my clumsy way, He was already preparing a very special gathering for me.

Seven Special Women

The day had arrived. The doorbell rang. The first of the seven women I had invited to my home was standing outside, waiting for me to find the courage to open the door. Had I ever been this nervous and scared? If I had, I couldn't recall when. Yet I knew this was my next step of obedience.

When I began noticing these women, I knew God was pointing them out to me for a reason. I was about to discover the vital role they would play in my journey. God had chosen these women for me to share my heart with. They were of various ages, in different stages of life, and from all walks of life. They were all believers but from different faiths and denominations. We were different in many ways, but, as we were about to find out, we were all alike in many other ways.

As I said, I had invited these women for coffee as an act of obedience. But now I stood at the door and silently cried out to God, "I can't do it! I really cannot do this!" I could not find the strength to pull open my front door. I stood trembling, afraid—and then I remembered my "cloud of witnesses," one of whom was Mother. In her final moments, she had found the courage to break through her fears and be vulnerable and transparent with me. Absent her strength, I would have been denied all that her truth had brought into my life. This woman I had for so long regarded as weak, God now held before me as an inspiration of strength. Once I'd thought I wanted to be nothing like her; that day, God gave me another little blessing. As I felt the knob turning and my own strength opening the door, I realized He had shown me that I did, in fact, want—and need—to be like my mother.

The Walls Come Down

One by one, the women arrived. We poured coffee, grabbed pastries, and gathered in the living room. We chatted and laughed as we always had. Then, as nervous and fearful as I could be, I began to really talk to them. I told them of my new journey and how I needed help. I shared how I felt God had hand-chosen them, and how I was simply trying to be obedient. I revealed my desire to grow, learn, and become a godly woman. I explained how I felt God had identified godly attributes within each of them that I needed to emulate.

"I don't know how to do that," I said. "I don't know how to get what you all have! I don't know how to become that woman. I don't even know where to begin unless you all can show me the way." Tears streamed down my face. I could see their shock. Until that moment, I had always led the way, been the teacher, been the one who took charge.

"You think you know me," I continued, "and in many ways you do. But today, I want you to know as much about the real me as I know." I went on to describe what had happened on that seventh step of my home. I had borrowed cardboard bricks from a preschool teacher to use as a visual. With one brick at a time, I built a wall around me, signifying all the "stuff" I had kept hidden away in my heart far too long. I wanted them to see each hurt, each question, each fear I carried as the bricks formed a wall between the world and me. I shared how until that day, when I had truly sensed Jesus passing by, I had lived each day trying to prove that my life was OK when I knew it was not. I confessed how I had come to be reconciled with the sad truth that I was not OK, but clung to the hope that I could be.

I told them the steps I had already taken to begin my journey to being OK. First, I had renewed my relationship with Jesus. I had been honest with my husband. I was following in Peter and

Jeremiah's instructional footsteps. The "ridding" and "reconciliation" process came next, and I shared each step that I knew I needed to take. I described how I was "running" with each step and letting God chart my course.

"Today," I said to them, "the walls come down!" I stood up and literally stepped through that wall! I believed with everything in me that as I did my part, God would do His!

That's Me, Folks

Silence. I looked around at the astonished faces of seven women who had known me for years but had never known the real me. Now, standing among the scattered cardboard bricks, I had broken through the façade and introduced the real me. My earlier trepidation paled in comparison to my new sense of relief and peace. I had been obedient. I had taken a huge step on my newly chosen path.

> *My transparency had given other women permission to share themselves truthfully.*

I had anticipated astonishment. I had even anticipated losing some friends. But I was unprepared for their tears. My transparency had given the other women permission to share themselves truthfully. The tears I saw that morning were from my friends being unmasked. The tears soon gave way to honest conversation about hurts in their lives. How ironic! Moments before, I had thought I was the only one—they had all seemed perfect to me. I had been so intimidated at how they had it all together in contrast to my own shortcomings! Yet even while possessing the godly attributes I had observed, each woman also battled her own burdens. That morning, those burdens came into the light.

Our group of seven soon discovered blessings growing from

the burdens we carried. Perhaps the biggest blessing: we were no longer happy with our spiritual status quo! And we were committed to help one another do something about it. Gone were the breezy chats about our occupations, our children, our husbands, our social calendars, our wardrobes; as we continued to meet weekly we deliberately chose to discuss only those things we had never openly talked about before.

Alone and Lonely

Looking back, I know I was naïve to think I was the only woman carrying great burdens through life. But be honest—have you been thinking the same thing? If so, it's time to embrace the truth. We have all made mistakes, we have hurt others, we have been hurt by others. Horrific tragedies have touched us; our dreams have been shattered. We struggle financially or physically, emotionally or spiritually. We have been unable to escape the voices of our past and their messages of unworthiness and insignificance. No, I am not the only woman who carried these burdens. You are not the only woman carrying such burdens.

> *The longer we believe we are alone in the world, the heavier our burden becomes.*

The longer we believe we are alone in the world, however, the heavier our burden becomes. It's as if the enemy backs us into a corner with his lies and shrouds all our thoughts in darkness so we cannot see any light. And we retreat still further into a very lonely place. Isolated. Deceived.

Yet we have to keep going. That's what good women do. Right? Our only option is to put on a happy face and proclaim, "Oh, I'm just fine. And you?" Days become weeks, and weeks become months. Before we know it, the months have become years, and we look into the mirror and wonder what happened. Who are we? When and where did we lose our true selves? Is it too late to fulfill what we were born to do? Is it possible to reconnect to that person we were before the hurts?

What our little group discovered once we told each other the truth is that we all had similar questions. We all believed similar lies. We discovered that none of us felt OK. We discovered that all of us longed for a hope to cling to. And we discovered that "just talking about it" helps.

Why "Just Talking" Works

As we openly discuss our burdens, our struggles and temptations, our hurts and our dreams, we begin to see how similar the heart of our situations can be. While we may read 1 Peter 5:9, which tells us we are not alone in our struggles and that others undergo the same hardships, we cannot buy into the truth of that verse if our eyes tell us that everyone has it together except us. We can't always rely on what we see, however. Honest dialogue—just talking—reveals what the eyes cannot: that we are not the only ones dealing with fears, guilt, regret, pain. "Just talking" reveals that while our enemy may be clever, he is not very creative; he uses the same tricks on all of us.

> While our enemy may be clever, he is not very creative; he uses the same tricks on all of us.

As I discovered firsthand the power of just talking, I couldn't help but wonder about my mother. What if—in all of her Bible studies, all of her Sunday school classes—one person had broken the silence and talked about her burdens? How might my mother's life have been different? How much sooner might the walls of pretending that imprisoned her have come tumbling down, releasing her to be who God had created her to be? How might God have used her to make an impact in her world?

I believe the world is full of silently hurting people. They are you and me and almost all those who surround us. They see you in church, sit next to you in Bible study, admire you when they see you at community functions. They attend PTO with you, live next door to you, and hug you after choir practice. They may be your sister or your daughter, your best friend or your mother. You seem so perfect to them.

They could never imagine the hurts you have suffered or are now walking through. They would never believe you live with your own secrets. Your great cover-up makes them doubt you could have ever sinned or made a mistake. Their admiration for you makes them feel inferior. They know their sins, their mistakes, their past, and their struggles, but they don't know yours. And so they wear masks.

Their hope is that someone—anyone—will break the silence. They need desperately for someone to show them that God accepts and has plans even for the imperfect, the unlovable, the mess-ups, the sinful, the ones who have been mistreated or endured abuse, the ones who have abused, the ones who live each day trying to prove they are OK. They need for one person to remove her mask so they can remove theirs.

As much as I needed those seven special women, I found to my great surprise that they also needed me. We needed to break the silence, to break the strongholds of isolation and loneliness, and begin honest dialogue. Only then could our burdens transform into blessings.

Stepping Out

As we conclude this chapter, I want to remind you of a powerful truth from the last chapter. Deuteronomy 30:11–14 says:

Now what I am commanding you today is not too difficult for you or beyond your reach. It is not up in heaven, so that you have to ask, "Who will ascend into heaven to get it and proclaim it to us so we may obey it?" Nor is it beyond the sea, so that you have to ask, "Who will cross the sea to get it and proclaim it to us so we may obey it?" No, the word is very near you; it is in your mouth and in your heart so you may obey it. (NIV)

What is God telling you to do? What is the next step? Who is He asking you to "just talk" to? This chapter has been about obedience. It has been about seeking God's face, surrendering to His purposes for you, and—when all is said and done—saying yes to whatever He shows you to do. Obedience can be hard, but Deuteronomy insists it is not beyond our reach. What is within your reach to do today to transform your burdens into blessings?

MAKE IT YOURS

It's Your Move

1. We commonly refer to decision points as crossroads. You'll recall that the Samaritan woman reached a crossroad and was forced to make a choice. What was her crossroad, and what choice did she make? What about my mother at her final crossroad—what do you recall about her choice?

2. What three principles did you see from Peter's life that guide us in the process of discovering our next steps? Where are you in this process?

3. Jeremiah 6:16 provides four principles for approaching crossroads in life. What are they? Where are you in this process?

4. Review the rainbow of promises from this chapter. What does "Roy G. Biv" stand for (besides the colors of the rainbow)?

5. Which of these promises speaks to your deepest need right now?

6. Why can we be confident that God's promises are not mere "ads" but rather something solid we can count on during each step we take of trust and obedience?

7. This week as you stand at your own crossroads with your brown bag in hand, you may be feeling pretty vague about your next steps. In this chapter, I identified four Rs from Hebrews 12:1 that can help us discern our next step. What are those four Rs?

8. Now let's make each R personal, beginning with **renewal.** Perhaps you already feel renewed and encouraged by my mom's crossroad story or that of the Samaritan woman. Do you have a more personal story that also encourages you to take your next step? Is there someone whose life gives you hope for what God can do to transform your burden?

9. Now let's personalize **ridding.** What hinders you from taking the next step toward blessing? What one thing pops into your mind that you need to get rid of? Is it doubt or a specific fear? Is it a habit robbing you of time or discipline? What do you need to say "good riddance" to so that you can move forward?

10. **Reconciliation** is the next R. Is there someone you need to talk to, send a card to, or take the first steps toward making amends with? Does someone need your honesty? Your forgiveness?

11. The final R is **running.** The word is a call to action. It carries a sense of urgency. Are you willing to run toward your opportunity today, or are you still holding back?

12. Read Deuteronomy 30:11–14 again. Taking the next step toward healing may seem impossible, but God tells us it is not beyond our reach. Take a moment to review your answers to this week's questions. Talk about them with God in prayer. Then summarize here what you believe God is saying to you about your next step. Remember, it may be a baby step, well within your reach. The key is, it's your move . . . and your time starts *now*!

Have You Met the Promise Maker?

In this chapter I talked a lot about God's promises as found in the Bible and how they helped me take the first steps toward transforming my burdens into blessings. But promises mean little to us if we've never met the Promise Maker. Have you met the Promise Maker? You may say, "I think so" or "I sure hope so," but God wants you to be able to say, "I know so." He has a made a way so that we can know for certain! "The Spirit himself testifies with our spirit that we are God's children" (Romans 8:16 NIV).

Are you assured of your salvation? Do you know with confidence that you are part of God's family, one of His beloved children? If you are unsure, open your Bible and think through the following Scripture passages.

"All have sinned and fall short of the glory of God."
(Romans 3:23 NIV)

"The wages of sin is death, but the gift of God is eternal life in Christ Jesus our Lord." (Romans 6:23 NIV)

"God demonstrates his own love for us in this:
While we were still sinners, Christ died for us."
(Romans 5:8 NIV)

"If you declare with your mouth, 'Jesus is Lord,' and believe in your heart that God raised him from the dead, you will be saved." (Romans 10:9 NIV)

If you read these passages and realize that you believe them but have never actually confessed your sin and accepted Jesus as your Savior, you can do so wherever you are right now. Pray your own prayer or use this one as an example to follow:

Dear Heavenly Father,

It's me. Thank You for Your love. Thank You for promising to turn Your ear toward me whenever I call Your name. I call on You today, Father, because I realize I have sinned and have fallen short of Your glory. I know that the wages of my sin is death. But I also know that even in my sin, I was so loved that You gave Your only son, Jesus, so that if I believed in Him I could have eternal life.

Dear Father, even though I do not understand it all, and even though I have questions, I do believe that Your Son died in my place for my sins! And I invite You, Jesus, into my heart and into my life as my Lord and as my Savior. Thank you for the new life You have promised, and I ask for assurance that I now belong to You. Amen

(If you made this decision, won't you please let me know? E-mail me at kim@rosesandrainbows.org)

Journal Notes

CHAPTER SIX

Embrace Today's Opportunities

Make the most of every opportunity.
—Ephesians 5:16 (NLT)

Throughout this study, we have seen that life events—whether seemingly insignificant or horrifically heartbreaking—can, through God's power, yield some of our greatest blessings. It is not that He nullifies our losses and our heartbreaks; rather God finds usefulness within our devastation by gifting it with meaning and purpose. He doesn't make it go away; He transforms it. We see the truth of this in the life of the Samaritan woman, in Abraham, and in countless others. Let me tell you another such story.

The College Professor

It was 1995, and I had just completed one of my first out-of-state speaking engagements in a church near a major university. As I walked off the platform, I was amazed at the number of women who lingered to talk to me. Grabbing some water, I sat on the top step while woman after woman described the hurt, regret, and abandoned dreams from some tragedy or mistake in her life.

Eventually, the line dwindled. I was about to leave when I saw another woman headed toward me, someone I had noticed lingering at a distance. Her body language and accusatory smirk gave me a glimpse of the pain she carried and prepared me for her abruptness. "I cannot accept this!" she declared. "I cannot believe, one, that God really cares—and two, that even if He could He would take a devastating and demoralizing sin and create something 'greater than we could imagine' as you say!" I could immediately see that whatever she'd done, she was convinced it was beyond God's desire or ability to transform.

"It's not about the sin," I responded. "We have all sinned . . . " That's as far as I got before she harshly interrupted. She had heard it all before. "But my sin is so much bigger!" she cried out. "And I have lived with it every day and in the darkness of every night for more than thirty years. No one knows. I have never told anyone."

Looking into this woman's eyes, I saw the destruction wrought by an enemy who isolates the hurting, the lonely, and the vulnerable to kill, steal, and destroy lives. My heart ached for her as I invited her to continue. Searching my face as if deciding whether to trust me, she finally blurted it out. "An abortion! No one knows, but I had an abortion!"

I held her as she sobbed. Thirty long years of guilt, pain, self-condemnation, personal disgust, and censure were being purged from her heart. She acknowledged she was a believer, and our discussion revealed she had experienced God's forgiveness. But she had been unable to rid her mind of the past. She could not forget.

And I knew why. God did not want her to forget! He had a purpose for her and was using this pain to lead her into that purpose. Certainly He wanted her to "throw off everything that hindered" her—the guilt, the condemnation—and the sins that were entangling her—the anger, the self-deprecation—but just as certainly He did not want her to forget what she had done. God saw something that she couldn't see: the story of His grace and comfort that she could take to so many other women contemplating or living with this same issue. This is what Paul spoke of in 2 Corinthians 1:3–4 when he called God "the God of all comfort, who comforts us in all our troubles, so that we may comfort those in any trouble with the comfort we ourselves receive from God" (NIV)

Only Jesus knew the personal and unique ministry that was within this professor. As she broke years of silence and spoke about her abortion, she unlocked the stronghold her secret had imposed. As she stepped into truth that day, she also stepped beyond that which had held her captive for more than three decades. The burden that had been safely tucked away in the darkness of her heart had suddenly been thrust into the light. Jesus had passed by, not only to bring truth but also to bring healing and opportunity.

I challenged her to quit running and confront her hurt. I invited her to begin the journey I had begun years before by first renewing her relationship with Jesus, and then facing her mirror. I challenged her to begin to rid herself of the negative thoughts that entangled her. Next I urged her to seek reconciliation where needed, and then to run with urgency to take whatever step God asked of her. I encouraged her to find friends—a friend—she could trust through each step of the journey. And finally I asked her to consider sharing her story. Not on the street corners, or just for the sake of proving she could do it, but when God handed her an opportunity—or two, or three. "Look around," I challenged her. "Where better could God have placed you than on a college campus where so many face a decision like yours and need the counsel you could provide?"

About six months later, I received a beautiful message from my new friend. She had begun helping women who'd had abortions come to terms with their choices as well as assisting coeds to find alternatives. To my knowledge, she is still doing so today. This, my friends, is how burdens become blessings! Once she completed her truth with God's truth, forgave herself, and stepped out on her own rainbow of God's promises, she found ongoing healing for herself and the thrill of offering God's hope to those He placed before her. What an amazing God we serve! From imprisoned to impassioned—that's what our God can do!

Think about this: No one heard the clanging of handcuffs or ankle weights falling away as the college professor was freed from all that held her. No one heard the creak of the prison doors opening, allowing her to walk free. Her prison was imaginary, though no less real in its devastation. Her prison existed only in her mind, where the enemy had planted his lies. Those lies had deafened her to Jesus' words from the cross: "It is finished" (John 19:30 NIV). He had completed all that His Father had sent Him to do, including "[proclaiming] freedom for the prisoners . . . to set the oppressed free" (Luke 4:18–19 NIV).

Does that mean our sin doesn't matter? Paul asks and answers that question in Romans 6:1–2: "What shall we say, then? Shall we go on sinning so that grace may increase? By no means" (NIV). Our sin matters so much, in fact, that Jesus died to pay its penalty. But His payment—and the resurrection power that followed—means God can use our sins, ugly as they are, for His perfect purposes.

The professor shows us the way to the next step. Once she moved into the light of truth with her burden, she was ready to embrace the opportunities God had for her. I believe you're ready for that next step too! But there may be a few obstacles to overcome first.

Busy Is Not Always Better

In the chapter "Seize God's Timing," we saw how procrastination hinders us from embracing what God wants to do in and for us.

It's not that we don't plan to do what He is asking, and it's not necessarily that we don't *want* to do what God asks. But we have these lengthy to-do lists that rule our hours and days, and it seems impossible to squeeze in all that we need to get done. God—being invisible and patient—is easy to keep moving to the bottom of the list. And we excuse our Godward procrastination by claiming we are waiting on God when, in fact, it is God who waits on us!

I often wonder how many opportunities and blessings I have missed by being so distracted by busyness. There's an old saying, "If the devil can't make you bad, he will make you busy!" Have you also experienced the truth of that saying? I want to propose a better way to live. Instead of overscheduling our lives, creating a breeding ground for procrastination, how about we challenge ourselves with Ephesians 5:16: "Make the most of every opportunity" (NLT) and tack on Hebrews 3:13 for good measure: "as long as it is called 'Today'" (NIV). Make the most of every opportunity as long as it is called "Today."

Knowing how we women are, I think we'd better add one small phrase to that mandate: make the most of every *God-given* opportunity as long as it is called "Today." Many of us end up with ridiculous to-do lists and the paralyzing habit of procrastination because we think every opportunity is ours to embrace. But I'd like us to focus on a particular kind of opportunity right now— the kind that God has custom-designed to fit the lives we have lived, complete with pain and failures and missteps and those heavy, heavy burdens. I'm talking about opportunities like those God handed the professor and that allowed her to take the most painful experience of her life and use it to bless others.

Here's another opportunity of a similar nature: think back to the woman I met in the grocery store not long after Mother died. She's probably not even aware that she seized a God-given opportunity that day. She simply showed compassion and care by asking how I was. Yet her sincerity broke through my façade, sent me running to my car in tears, and eventually jump-started my journey toward becoming OK.

I can't help but wonder: What if her to-do list had been too long that day to allow a brief word with me? What if she had said to herself, *I'll say something to Kim later?*

That's why I believe busyness is one of our biggest obstacles to seeing our burdens transformed into blessings. It might make us feel important and good about ourselves. It might distract us from the pain and disappointment we carry in our hearts. But busyness also prevents us from experiencing the transformation God wants to bring about in and through us as we embrace opportunities He brings our way.

Bad Stuff Is Good Stuff

Another obstacle for many of us is a lie we believe. We think God can only use the good stuff in our lives.

I've already told you how that obstacle robbed my mother of a lifetime of blessings. Because she did not have a flawless past, free of mistakes and regrets, she had been deceived into believing she was unusable to God. She was convinced she had nothing to offer Him.

As we share our brokenness and imperfections, we allow others to see that God is not limited by "bad stuff" in our lives.

Such thinking is utterly wrong. God does not think that way. He can and does use our successes, talents, and gifts, but He also uses our hurts and burdens for His good purposes. In fact, it's most often our pain that people can relate to, and where they find hope. As we share our brokenness and imperfections, we allow others to see that God is not limited by "bad stuff" in our lives. He is not limited by imperfection. As a matter of fact, He says He will use those things that are not wise, not influential, not of noble birth (1 Corinthians 1:26). He chooses "the foolish things of the world . . . the weak things of the world to shame the strong . . . the lowly things of this world and the despised things—and the things that are not . . . so that no one may boast before him" (verses 27–29 NIV).

I know this is contrary to human reasoning and logic. No wonder we get stuck here. But we need to get unstuck! Because our churches are full of wonderful, unfulfilled women (and men) who feel—and who may be viewed as if—they have nothing to offer God.

I remind you of the Samaritan woman. Not a pillar of the community. No connections. Shady past (divorced!). Shady present, for that matter (living with a man!). Who among the spiritual could imagine that she would be Jesus's first choice to testify of God's unconditional love and acceptance?

I hope you are having a spiritual "ah-ha" moment right about now. I pray the light of hope within your heart is coming on. I pray you are beginning to see that God's power to use what you have to offer goes way beyond your rational thinking. No amount of human knowledge can comprehend or limit God's ability. No bad stuff from your past (or your future) can get in His way of doing great things in your life.

Where's Your Focus?

A third obstacle that keeps many of us from believing God can use us is closely related to the one we just discussed. One reason we get hung up on the bad stuff in our lives is that we are focused in the wrong direction. So I ask you: Where's your focus?

When I was young, I was sure Mother and Daddy had eyes in the back of their heads that gave them the ability to see what was going on behind them. As I grew up, I seemed to share that same feature in that I was overly focused on what was behind me—my past. I saw only what had been and was not looking ahead. In addition, I viewed my past only from one perspective—my own—instead of seeking God's perspective. As a result, I could not make peace with my past; I could not let go of what "should have been." This backward focus blinded me to God's promises for my future.

You see, though I had worked through many of the abandonment, abuse, and distrust issues of my past, another issue had emerged in my adulthood: my conviction that God had betrayed me by not answering my prayers and taking Mother from me when she and I had finally reconciled and were enjoying one another. At a time in my life when God was beckoning me, calling me into new chapters with new meaning, I was struggling with this piece of the past. But as God persisted in drawing near to me, and as I spent more time in His Word—with His promises, getting His perspective—my focus began to change. Rather than seeing Mother as "gone," I began to see her as "given." Though her time on this earth was not as long as I would have wished, it was the time she had been allotted by her loving Father. I still didn't like it. I still wished she were just a phone call away. But I grew convinced that God intended to honor her—and use me—through both her life and death, and that began to motivate me to look forward, not backward, to embrace the opportunities He was about to set before me.

It's a Stretch

I've described three major obstacles I've encountered that could have prevented me from embracing opportunities from God. Your obstacles may be different from mine. I encourage you to examine yourself and identify what's standing in your way. Whatever our personal obstacles may be, this next truth is the same for all of us: we must stretch beyond our comprehension, our abilities, our past, our perspective—beyond our losses, frailty, and weaknesses—to be what God wants us to be and to do what He calls us to do.

I have a box of rubber bands I keep in my office. I look at them often and think of us. Yes, you and me. My rubber bands are all sizes, just like us; and they are all colors, just like us. And they all have to stretch to do what they were made to do. Again, just like us. We cannot reach our full potential until we are stretched.

You Are There

Maybe you're now thinking, *I've acknowledged that God views me differently from how I view myself. He sees potential and promise in the things I hate most about myself—the pain I bear, the shame I feel, the burdens that weigh me down. He is ready and eager to make my life count—yes, my messy life. His vision for me is one of opportunity and meaningfulness. I get that. My heart is ready. But I have no idea where to start.*

> *The place and the work God has for us is right where we are today.*

I heard this statement on the radio the other day: "Just be where you are!" What a profound, yet exquisitely simple, idea. How many of us realize that the place and the work God has for us is right where we are today? Do we understand that our opportunities are tucked into what we may deem ordinary, everyday moments: as we talk to a coworker, or hear a child appealing for attention, or gather at the dinner table? Awareness of this truth brings a renewed purpose to each day and significance to individual daily encounters.

So here it is: you start where God has placed you. Just like the professor. Just like the woman in the grocery store. Just like the Samaritan woman. Stop where you are (that might mean letting go of some of your busyness). Open your eyes to see (that might mean yanking your focus away from the past). Open your ears to listen. God is showing you what to do next.

Are you getting a little frustrated because I'm not telling you exactly what opportunities to seize and how to seize them? There's no formula for *how* God will transform your burdens into blessings. He doesn't operate in a tight little box, never deviating to the left or right. No, His ways are as varied as His creation. He doesn't make any two people exactly alike, and I suspect He doesn't have any identical plans for His people. He is ever creating. Our job is to notice what He is creating and where and with whom. That's the discernment part. I love this prayer in Psalm 119:125: "I am your servant; give me discernment that I may understand" (NIV).

Hearing Aids

When you invite God to give you discernment, you start to discover that one person's silence is really a scream for help. Another person's cruel words are really the bleeding from a painful wound. All those "together" people who surround you are carrying burdens much like your own. And God has you in mind to help Him bring blessing from those burdens.

I reminded you just a few paragraphs ago that embracing God's opportunities would require stretching. One reason that's true is that God is calling you to reach out to hurting people (is there any other kind?), and hurting people hurt people. A person's judgmental or mean-spirited ways may be the avenue God uses to reveal who needs love and kindness the most. That's where discerning eyes and ears come into the picture (a thick skin is helpful too!).

God has brought many hurting people into my life over the years, and they all have this in common: they need to be listened to. I try to listen beyond the obvious in three ways:

(1) I listen to what is being said;
(2) I listen to what the speaker is not saying; and
(3) I listen to the nudging of the Holy Spirit.

I recall so vividly one instance when using these three dimensions of listening saved me and another woman from a lot of hurt feelings.

Having moved to a new area, Lee and I had joined a small church that had no women's ministry. I saw firsthand how God puts you where your passion lies. I pulled out the manuals I had written during my times of stumbling through women's ministry in the past, rolled up my sleeves, and off I went.

Things were moving along at a gallop. The ladies were enthused, the pastor approved, and I was up to my eyeballs in sheer joy. I began with some one-shot topical events. I had just concluded one such event when I saw a woman approaching me with a look on her face that told me she wanted to spit at me.

"I don't like you, and I probably never will," she said. I waited for a laugh, a smile, anything to let me know she was only kidding, but there was nothing before me but a stone-cold face.

Years before, these words could have paralyzed me and sabotaged any good work I felt God doing. But facing my own hurt had helped me understand that hurtful people are that way because they hurt too. I began to pray silently, "Lord, I hear what she is saying, please help me to understand what she is not ready or willing to say. Please allow Your Holy Spirit to guide and give me wisdom." Then I turned my attention to this fireball of a woman.

It took more than one conversation to get to the real truth, but as it turns out, it wasn't me that this lady did not like. It was the fact that God was using me in a way she had always wanted to be used. I represented the opportunity she felt she had lost.

Because I listened both to what was said and what was not said, and relied on insight from the Holy Spirit, our talks remained free of anger, accusation, and judgment. A potentially damaging confrontation became a divine opportunity. This woman became my spiritual sidekick and my friend, and two years later she became the women's ministry leader in that church. That's the power of discerning listening.

Seeing the Unseen

Seeing what no one else can see, hearing what others cannot hear: this is probably different from any other description of "doing" that you have heard, but it is the way of God's kingdom. Paul, a powerful servant in God's kingdom, wrote, "We fix our eyes not on what is seen, but what is unseen" (2 Corinthians 4:18 NIV).

The FedEx logo gives a down-to-earth glimpse of what I'm talking about. We've all seen it, right? But have you ever noticed the arrow in the logo? Most people don't at first, but look closely between the e and the x in "ex."

Once you see the arrow, your eyes are conditioned to go there every time. It is the same with the people and circumstances we face each day: the grumpy cashier, the teacher who yells at your child, the loud lady beside you at baseball games, the person conducting your job interview, the nurse administering the chemotherapy you endure. Hidden within every one of these places, people, and circumstances are opportunities to join God in His ministry of healing and hope. When we embrace this kingdom reality, we grow progressively sensitized to the multitudes that bump against us as we go about our busy, busy lives. Our eyesight grows sharper, our hearing more acute. No longer do we sit in our corner and wonder when God will use us; now we see opportunities for good work everywhere we look! Welcome to the world of discernment.

Who needs your encouragement today? Will you ask God to give you discerning eyes and discerning ears to see and hear what others around you are missing? Will you ask the Holy Spirit to show you whom, among the multitudes, He wants you to reach out to? And then will you embrace that opportunity?

Seven Words That Will Change Your Life

You might be saying, "I have tried this before. It just doesn't work for me. Besides, I'm exhausted from all the other demands on me." I understand. I have felt the same way at times. This story from Peter's life, however, has helped me weather seasons of feeling overwhelmed. His words motivate and inspire me daily.

> One day as Jesus was standing by the Lake of Gennesaret, the people were crowding around him and listening to the word of God. He saw at the water's edge two boats, left there by the fishermen, who were washing their nets. He got into one of the boats, the one belonging to Simon [Peter], and asked him to put out a little from shore. Then he sat down and taught the people . . . When he had finished speaking, he said to Simon, "Put out into deep water, and let down the nets for a catch." Simon answered, "Master, we've worked hard all night and haven't caught anything. But because you say so, I will let down the nets." (Luke 5:1–5 NIV)

Peter was a professional fisherman and had tried catching fish over and over again that evening. Besides being exhausted, he was probably embarrassed: everyone else seemed to be catching all the fish. Discouraged, he was rolling in his nets and giving up. But Jesus passed by. He asked Peter to try one more time. In frustration, Peter acknowledged his own truth ("We've tried . . . I'm tired"), but he also acknowledged the one who had never let him down when he simply said, "But because you say so, I will."

"But because you say so, I will." These seven words have the potential to change our lives. Have they been your response in the past? If not, they can be your response starting this very minute!

Tucked within your burdens, a blessing may be a single decision away.

Tucked within your burdens, a blessing may be a single decision away. Because you are reading this book, I know you are looking for what God has tucked in the darkness of your circumstances. You are well aware of the burden; you are just wondering if there truly can be a blessing in it. Like me, you have probably tried to fill that emptiness and hurt with a lot of what the world has to offer. Maybe you were stuck and about to give up. I am so glad you haven't.

Will you get up each morning and ask God to give you ears to hear and eyes to see the opportunities He is putting before you? Will you commit to acting at the time you feel God is asking, no matter what it is? Will you confront your burdens and push beyond any temptations to feel embarrassed, or insecure, or surprised at whom God has called you to? Will you just obey?

Will you recognize it is not you, but God who will be faithful to complete the task? Will you give God permission to use your "good stuff" as well as all that seems wasted, hurtful, shameful, and painful? Will you stretch to what you were made to do by declaring, "But because you said so, I will"?

I'm reminded again of one of God's promises. Every time He invites us to do something in His kingdom, He gives us a promise as well: "He who began a good work in you will carry it on to completion" (Philippians 1:6 NIV). We make ourselves available, we embrace the opportunities, He does the work.

This is one way I visualize it: we are like ink pens; we are merely the writing instruments. God's eyes have rested upon us, He has chosen us, and His hand picks us up. He is the ink that flows through us and uses our lives to write His message to others around us and to fulfill His purposes. Yet He never uses us without asking our permission. He seeks *willing* instruments. That's love, don't you think?

Steps and Stories

How do we take all we've been learning—understanding that we all have hurts, believing God can transform them, recognizing His timing, choosing obedience—and apply it to today's opportunities?

I have come to rely on three steps to help me respond to opportunities God gives me. The first step is to *identify the situation*—that moment when I sense God is asking me to act. The second step is to *identify what He is asking of me*: to speak a kind word, to invite someone for coffee and a chat, to tell my story to someone in the same situation I was once in, and so on. And third: I just need to *go for it*, whatever it is, regardless of my comfort level or the messages playing my mind, in spite of my fear or embarrassment or whatever else makes me want to delay.

I've already talked about being overwhelmed by what God is asking. But another outcome when we receive an opportunity from God is to be "underwhelmed" or discouraged by how insignificant our calling is. We can heed the wisdom of Zechariah 4:10: "Do not despise these small beginnings" (NLT). God is concerned not with the size of the task but with the size of our obedience! In God's economy, "to obey is better than sacrifice" (1 Samuel 15:22 NIV). He is not concerned with showiness or grand gestures; He simply invites us to use what we have to be involved in what He is asking.

Along with these three steps—identifying the situation, identifying what God is asking of you, and going for it—God has given you an invaluable tool to use when embracing His opportunities. What tool? Your story. Yes, *your* story.

God intends to use your story for spreading His kingdom in the hearts of other women.

Throughout this book, you have seen God use my mother's hidden-burden story—first in my life and then in the lives of others. In this chapter, you saw God use the professor's story to help women who naturally came into her sphere of influence. You have a story too, and God intends to use it for spreading His kingdom in the hearts of other women. "But I don't know how to tell my story!" you are probably exclaiming right now. That's what I'm going to help you do next—through continued, focused journaling.

Don't let the word *journaling* scare you. You've been journaling since you began this study as you've answered the questions at the end of each chapter and made notes about what you've been reading. Simply put, I believe the best way to sort through your story is to write it down, and journaling allows you to do that reflectively, whenever God gives you insights, and with complete privacy. Your journal may be a three-ring binder, a leather-bound book, or your laptop. If you hate writing, if you freeze in frustration the moment you pick up a pen or sit down at your keyboard, then you might choose to dictate your "journal" into a digital recording device. The point is, start telling your story to yourself so you will be able to tell it to others who need to hear it.

As you've discovered already, your story will not write itself in a weekend. It has been unfolding during this study, and you'll find it continues to unfold over a long period of time. That's what happened for me. Some of my story fell into place when Mother passed away. Some fell into place when my sons were born. Other pieces became clear to me on ordinary days when I was driving to and from errands, or jogging and praying, or weeping in desperation. Don't rush the process, but don't give up on it either. Your story, burdens and all, is the most important tool you possess as you reach out to others. God will use your story to build bridges, bind broken hearts, reveal Himself to people who need Him, and so much more.

I also believe God will use your story the moment you offer it up to Him, crude and incomplete as it may be. I doubt that He plans to sit back and wait for your story to be so refined and polished it would win a Pulitzer. Long before you believe your story is ready for public consumption, God will be using "chunks" of your story to bring hope and blessings to others. The story of your botched music audition at age twenty-two may be the only part of your story that the woman sitting next to you in the airport needs to hear. It doesn't matter that you have fourteen more years of story to tell! The moment you start this storying process is the moment you embrace opportunities from God.

I used the word *focused* to describe your journaling because that is what this book and its study questions have been training you to do. Focus on you, your life experiences, your truths, what your mirror says, what's in your bag. I am going to suggest a number of questions to continue to guide your reflection. Remember, you are "reliving" your story so you can recognize the burdens God wants to turn into blessings for both you *and* someone else. Many of the questions I give you will sound intense: don't expect questions like "What's your favorite color?" Also, some of the questions I suggest will not immediately seem related to your story, but they are simply coming at your story from a different, less obvious angle. None of these questions are mandatory. They are guides to help you, and if they are not helpful you can ignore them. And please add questions of your own to stimulate your journaling; my list is far from exhaustive.

It's time to dive in. Time to embrace God's opportunities. Your sample journaling questions are right after this chapter's "Make It Yours" section. Go ahead, pick a question, and start writing!

MAKE IT YOURS

Opportunities Abound

1. What aspects, if any, of the professor's story did you identify with?

2. Busyness can prevent us from embracing opportunities God offers us. Yet responding to opportunities from God can also keep us busy. What do you think is the difference between busyness for the sake of busyness and busyness in response to God's urging?

3. Another obstacle to embracing God's opportunities is doubting that He can use the bad stuff in our lives to encourage or bless others. How has a specific promise from God, story from this study, or encouraging word from someone who knows you helped you move toward hope about the burden in your brown paper bag?

4. Many of us focus too much on the past or are crippled by fear of the future. What perspective does Philippians 3:7–14 encourage us to have?

5. Many times we think that grand gestures count more than small ones. How does Matthew 10:42 challenge this perspective?

6. You were challenged to take a "next step" last week. Was it like a "cup of water" or was it something that will take a while to unfold? Explain.

7. Which of these phrases best captures your reaction to writing out your story so God can use it as a blessing to others? (Be honest!)

   "It's too hard!"   "What fun!"

   "How exciting!"   "I'm tired just thinking about it."

   "My story is dull." "My story is too messy to help anyone."

   "I hate to write!"   "This is answered prayer."

   "I'll fail."   "I didn't sign on for this!"

   "I'm scared but   "I think this could turn my life
   I'll try."   around!"

8. Grabbing opportunities to reach out to others, writing your story so God can use it with other hurting people—these are daunting challenges. That's why the seven words of Peter are so important: "But because you say so, I will." What aspect of uttering these words to God scares you the most?

9. What aspect of saying these seven words to God excites you the most? Let yourself imagine how your life might change because you are courageous enough to say these seven words. If your imagination needs help, read Ephesians 3:20!

10. Let's pull out your brown paper bag again. I suspect that there was a time when you saw only your hurts when you looked in the mirror. Perhaps you dreamed of a different future but felt it was impossible. Now, seeing yourself through the lenses of God's promises and the encouraging words of those who really know you, can you see the possibilities of blessings? It's not easy, I know, but one step at a time the transition is happening. Look how far you have already come! Are you willing to commit at

an even deeper level this week? If you are, keep wearing that rubber band from last week. Whenever you feel stretched give it a tug to remind yourself that thousands of other women have also committed to letting God stretch them this week by using their burdens as blessings in another person's life. Then before you take the plunge—and follow the arrow—whisper a prayer of thanks to God that He uses stretching experiences to help us reach our full potential. If you will commit, write Peter's seven words on your bag under your dash.

Telling Your Story

ere are questions and guidelines to help you flesh out your story. Use any that are helpful and feel free to ignore the rest.

- Describe your family during your childhood: your parents, siblings, any family stories and legends that shaped you, where you lived, and so on.

- What are some of the best memories of your childhood? Your teens? When you look back at that season, what makes you smile? Don't just describe what happened but dig into what made these memories so good.

- Who are the people you remember most fondly from your childhood? Your teens? What made each person so appealing to you?

- Who from your childhood (and/or teens) left the strongest mark on you (positive or negative)? Whose influence continues to determine your actions and reactions today?

- How would you complete this sentence: As a little girl, I would have never guessed this would happen to me . . .

- What hurtful words do you still remember from your childhood and/or teen years?

- What are the most affirming words you remember from your childhood? Your teen years?

- What tragedies do you recall from your childhood? How did they affect you at the time? Do they still affect you today?

- What do you wish you could change about your early years?

- What's the earliest memory you have of masking your emotions (pain, anger, hurt, disappointment, etc.)? How did you do this (body language, humor, withdrawal, etc.)?

- Who are the key people you blame for the burdens you bear today? Who do you hold accountable for the hurt?

- What life issues have emerged from your efforts to escape or mask your pain? (If you remember, mine included anorexia, diet pill addictions, and depression, among others.)

- What glimpses have you had of how Jesus might want to use your life?

- What doubts have plagued you over the years?

- What fears do you wrestle with? Can you identify when those fears first began or what triggered them?

- What Scriptures, maxims, mottos, or philosophies have shaped your attitude toward your life? (For example: "Jesus loves me." "Time heals all wounds." "She who has the most toys wins." "Grin and bear it." "Big girls don't cry." "All things work together for good.")

- Do you have a personal relationship with God? If so, how did that come about? What difference has it made in your life, if any?

- Who has been the most trustworthy person in your life?

- Who has betrayed your trust?

- Who is the most encouraging person in your life? What do they do to encourage you?

- Who brings you down whenever you are with that person? Why is that?

- How surprised would most people be by the burdens you are carrying?

- What is the greatest hurt of your life? When did this occur? Describe the event: people involved, where you were, what it did in your life.

- What is the greatest joy in your life? Why does this person or circumstance or event bring you such joy?

- What are your biggest relational obstacles (fear, distrust, shyness, hunger for approval, etc.)? Can you trace the origin of that relational behavior?

- In what ways have you been disillusioned about God? How do you feel He has let you down?

- What people have let you down the most in life? How has that influenced your behavior?

- What lies do you tell yourself? Where did that thinking originate—a person, event?

- What is your biggest obstacle to moving forward in life with joy and purpose? How long has that obstacle been there? When did you first notice it? What steps have you taken to try to get past it?

Journal Notes

CHAPTER SEVEN

Never Give Up!

Keep up your courage, for I know it will be
just as God has declared it will be!
—Acts 27:25 (paraphrased)

Once there was an ugly brown bag. Actually, in the story I'm about to tell, the bag was probably a basket, but a humble one just as the brown bags we've talked about in this book are humble. But I'm getting ahead of myself. Let's backtrack a little bit and set the scene properly:

> Jesus crossed to the far shore of the Sea of Galilee . . . and a great crowd of people followed him because they saw the signs he had performed by healing the sick. Then Jesus went up on a mountainside and sat down with his disciples. The Jewish Passover Festival was near. When Jesus looked up and saw a great crowd coming toward him, he said to Philip, "Where shall we buy bread for these people to eat?" He asked this only to test him, for he already had in mind what he was going to do.
>
> Philip answered him, "It would take more than half a year's wages to buy enough bread for each one to have

a bite!" Another of his disciples, Andrew, Simon Peter's brother, spoke up, "Here is a boy with five small barley loaves and two small fish, but how far will they go among so many?" (John 6:1–9 NIV)

By now it's clear that Jesus is asking His disciples to do something impossible. There were more than five thousand men plus their wives and children, and all of them were famished. And among them, only one little boy had brought his "brown bag" lunch. I wonder if earlier that morning he had pleaded with his mom not to make him carry that lunch. Maybe he knew no one else would bring barley loaves and tiny fish to the event; they would surely eat at festive food booths! Might he have tucked his modest meal under his shirt, embarrassed and hoping others wouldn't see that he came from a family without the financial resources to eat out?

That part is merely speculation, but I am confident of this: the lad had all that was required; he had a heart for Jesus. I know this because when approached for the contents of his bag, he handed over all that he had. Jesus apparently needed his brown bag lunch, and he was happy to cooperate with Jesus. And once the boy turned his bag over to Jesus, Jesus transformed the contents. The embarrassingly humble meal became a feast that blessed a multitude.

Your Bag

In the beginning was another ugly brown bag—yours. It started out as an empty bag until I asked the rather confrontational question: What is in the bag that's eating at you? From that moment on, week by week and chapter by chapter, you filled your bag with burdens you've endured or longings you hold in your heart. You've been told more than once that God wants to take what is in your bag and transform it into blessings for both you and those around you. So as we arrive at our final chapter, I'm compelled to ask, "What has God been doing with the contents of your bag?"

Did you experience a blessing or two spilling from your bag of burdens? Or are you still hiding what's in your bag? Are the masks still firmly in place, the walls still standing? If so, I'm here to tell you one more time: God has called you to much more than a life of hiding and self-protection. He wants to work in your life in ways that may seem impossible to you but are a cinch for the God of the universe. He is in the process of spilling from that little bag of yours those things you have always deemed worthless and insignificant, those things that have been eating away at your heart, because He intends to use them to feed hope to the famished multitudes you walk among each day. God's perfect love plus your imperfect life add up to abundant blessings.

> God's perfect love plus your imperfect life add up to abundant blessings.

"If Only"

As one who has stood in a pit of great pain and disappointment filled with absolute hopelessness, from one who believed the lies of worthlessness and insignificance, from one who thought life could never be more than a masquerade, may I humbly, yet boldly and confidently, say to you, "Please, oh please, do not settle for anything less than God's best for your life!"

I won't pretend it will be easy; I hope I have made that clear by now. For one thing, you have an enemy who is trying to pile up so many lies in front of you that you can't see God standing front and center, offering you an incredible future. We have to remember, however, that we have been empowered through Christ not to be deceived (James 1:16). As the enemy whispers lies to you today, your privilege is to tell him, "Just hush up!" Remember, Jesus describes your enemy this way: "He was a murderer from the begining, not holding to the truth, for there is no truth in him . . . He is a liar and the father of lies" (John 8:44 NIV). We can wield this information as an effective weapon in our continuous battle for our future.

Meanwhile, we can count on our enemy to wield his weapon of "if onlys" against us. Think about that for a minute. How many nights have you lain in bed, unable to sleep, oppressed by regrets for how life might have been? For many years, that was my life. I lived hemmed in by "if onlys" and didn't even recognize it. My "if onlys" were all my excuses, all my declarations of what "could have been" but could no longer be because of the past.

- If only . . . I had not been taken from my grandparents.
- If only . . . I had matured and developed in a loving environment.
- If only . . . I had been strong enough not to let those things hurt me.
- If only . . . I could be good enough.
- If only . . . I could be pretty enough, skinny enough, smart enough.

These "if onlys" drained me of hope and chained me to my past. But God showed me a better way to respond to my past and embrace my future.

What If

The flip side to the "if onlys" the enemy throws your way are the "what ifs" of God's promises.

- What if God's promises are true not only for the Samaritan woman and Abraham but also for you and me?

- What if we truly believed God's promises? Would it matter in our lives?
- What if we seized our moment with God?
- What if we determined to do what we feel God is telling us to do right now, here, today?
- What if we began to see our lives not as a series of unfortunate circumstances and hurts but rather as perfect for God's use?
- What if we believed God was always working—not hurriedly or hastily, but deliberately and sometimes for years—with those He expects to use greatly?
- What if we believed God has been readying us as His instruments, allowing us to see His power, so that at His perfect moment we would be equal to every task for which He created us?
- What if we let our "if onlys" and our excuses become catalysts to finding the truth-bearing, life-altering, God-given confidence that the "what ifs" promise?
- And what if we learn to personalize, internalize, and build our lives upon those promises?

Wait, There's More

We've seen how the enemy tries to thwart us with "if onlys." We've seen that our "if onlys" can transform into "what ifs" as we discover the promises of God. But there's an even greater transformation ahead, and that's when the "what ifs" become "I know" statements about what is true in our lives.

What do you know for sure about you and God? Here's what I know:

I know God loves me as He says. I know He fearfully and wonderfully created me in my mother's womb. I know this because He says I am His workmanship.

I know I am loved so deeply that He gave His only begotten Son, Jesus, so that I could have abundant and eternal life with a plan and a purpose—beginning here, right where I am, right now.

I know His arms were the arms I had been trying to run to. I know He is the Daddy in whom I found assurance and acceptance. I know He proclaims, "I am the King of Kings and you, Kim, are My daughter!"

I know that by the power of His word I am transformed from mistake to majesty.

I know His blood is the seal of my adoption and His hand is the place of my security. I know "no one can snatch me from his hand" (John 10:28; personalized).

Remembering the Journey

And now it's your turn. This study has challenged you to probe your heart to examine profound hurts and devastations. You have faced your personal mirror and looked into the depths of your burdens. You have been challenged to stretch beyond your status quo. After all that, what do *you* know?

Chapter One asked you to dare to acknowledge your hurt. Given an ugly ol' brown bag, you were asked to identify what was in the bag that eats away at you. It has taken real courage for you to look at what lies heavy on your mind and heart. Had you been satisfied with your status quo, had you not already realized you were settling for less than God's best, had you chosen to play it safe, I would have lost you in the first chapter. But because you persevered, I know God smiled and said, "That's My girl!" I believe He knew then that you were tired of the lies and stood ready to do whatever was needed to discover His truth about your life. He knew you were ready to relinquish the burden in your bag and trade your "if onlys" for some new (and accurate!) "I knows."

In *Chapter Two* you were asked to become an Ephesians

3:20 woman who dares to believe that what God says about the transformation of your burdens to blessings can truly happen. You wrote "Glory be to God who, by His mighty power at work within me, can accomplish abundantly more than I could dare to ask or even imagine" on your brown bag. Though you've spent a lifetime listening to false promises and overblown claims, I urged you to take God at His word, even without visible evidence. What "I know" declarations can you now make about who God is, what His character is like, what He wants to do with your burdens? Where are you on your belief barometer compared to where you were several weeks ago?

Chapter Three challenged you to seize God's timing. Most of us have been admonished to wait on God's timing, but was the idea of seizing God's timing new to you? If you recall, I shared how if I had delayed my phone call to Mother, her perception of my motive for seeking reconciliation would have been entirely different. I also shared that faith did not make it easy to take the practical steps of obedience that God asked of me, but faith made it possible. What "I know" declarations are you ready to make about God's timing? What do you know for sure about how to hear God?

Whatever your truth says to you to limit you, God says, "You can be."

In *Chapter Four* you learned why it's important to fight for your future. The enemy has one version of "truth" that he uses to trick and tempt you. You have another version of "truth" that is tainted by your life experiences and your limited perception of those experiences. And then there's God's truth: that He takes all things—even those that make you feel the least worthy, the least OK—and helps you find a way to use them for your good and His glory. Whatever your truth says to limit you, God says, "You can be." When we grasp the reality of God's empowerment we began to see life as more than mere existence—breathing, speaking, enduring from one day to the next; we see our lives as abounding in joy, purpose, significance, and high-kicking excitement! What "I know" declarations are you ready to make about what you can be with God's help?

Chapter Five asked you to step out in faith—beyond your comfort level and preconceived notions of your abilities—onto your own rainbow of God's promises to discover what God can do through you. That chapter introduced you to the importance of other like-minded women in your life who could help you tear down the walls and push beyond the status quo into a richer, freer experience of God and His purposes. Were you able to begin sharing a part of you that no one in your group knew about?

Honestly, I have to stop right here to say this was not a study for the faint of heart! This study took guts—I know it and God knows it. Good for you for sticking with it and for wanting God's best. Here is what I know: with God, nothing—even the transformation of your burdens into blessings—is impossible. As you've taken your first steps forward, have you experienced a sense of peace and purpose like you have never known? Have you gotten reacquainted with yourself and found out that you like you? And have your friends stuck by you and loved you even more because they know you more? Are you able to make the same "I know" declaration that I just made: that with God nothing is impossible?

Chapter Six brought it all home by urging you to embrace today's opportunities. Situations you once deemed coincidental or even hurtful can now be opportunities God puts along your path. Embracing those opportunities requires discernment, attentiveness, engaging in the lives of those around you, and resolving like Peter that "because [Jesus] said so, I will." That resolve translates into huge blessings as you let God use the healed hurts in your life to give others hope for their healing. About what recent opportunity are you able to say, "I *know* that was from God and He used my burden to give _____ hope"?

Let God use the healed hurts in your life to give others hope for their healing.

We've just reviewed the "story" of where God has taken us through this book. But I still owe you another story: where God took me after His encounter with me on the seventh step of 509 Brandermill Road.

Roses and Rainbows

"Welcome to our first annual Roses and Rainbows Conference!"

It was another beautiful autumn morning. Trees glistened with changing colors. The air was crisp and cool. It had been thirty long years since a little princess had headed to her "palace" to play. Yet I felt as if I had found my way back to that little girl. My granddad's words, spoken as I dangled my little-girl legs from the porch swing, were in the forefront of my mind: "There is One, my little Kim, who loves you even more than I do." After all these years, I had found Him—or allowed myself to be found by Him. And from the solid foundation of His love, I had discovered who I am because of Him.

My pastor introduced me, and I looked out across the hundreds of women seated at West Acres Baptist Church that Saturday morning. I saw a church filled with women of all ages, all races, all denominations, all walks of life. Never could I have foreseen that the small group of seven women who met in my home each week would be used to influence a city and county in such a way!

Making my way onto the platform, I had glanced from one

woman to another, seeking familiar faces. Ah, there was the first woman to ring my doorbell on the day I knocked down the wall of cardboard blocks that imprisoned me. *Thank God for you*, I thought to myself as I recalled my struggle to summon the courage simply to open my front door. I still vividly remember this woman's beautiful and caring smile that settled my nerves and let me know I was OK. *Thank God that you came to my rescue!* I was acutely aware of how much I needed these people in my life and how stunted my journey had been when I tried to go it alone.

As I continued toward the platform, my heart was pounding so hard I glanced down to see if any chest palpitations were visible. As applause broke out, I felt a rush of embarrassment, and my nerves began to fray. For a moment, I reverted to my old pep talk: *Don't mess this up, Kim! Walk right, stand straight, head high. Smile, they're all looking at you!* Yet in the next instant I shrugged off my insecurities and negative thoughts in favor of the truth of God's Word. I found confidence to continue as I remembered, *Oh, I don't have to be perfect. That's God's job!*

My battle since leaving that seventh step had been a prolonged one, marked by a lot of tears. At times I felt my obedience had left me completely exposed and vulnerable. Other moments I felt foolish. Many, many times I just wanted to rebuild that wall around myself and give up! Thank God for Galatians 6:9, a passage that had been added to my repertoire of "print to practice" Scriptures: "Let us not become weary. . . . Do not give up" (NIV).

God wouldn't be counseling us not to grow weary had He not foreseen weariness in our future. I believe He recognizes that not growing weary or discouraged is a pretty tall order even for the most spiritual among us. He knows, without a doubt, we will face discouragement, and He is telling us what to do when it comes.

In this Scripture, I hear Him gently saying, "OK, Kim, just listen to Me. You are going to start a new journey on which I will ask you to do some uncomfortable things. Sometimes, even when you do what I ask, the results will not be immediate or turn out as you think they should. You may not have a rush of warm, fuzzy feelings; in fact, you may feel even more confused. You will have the urge to revert to your old thinking. You may want to throw up your hands and quit. Don't!" He continues, "Even though you can't see or understand all that is happening, I am working. The results will come. You just hang in there and never give up!"

I had hung in there, and this is where it had taken me: a ministry called Roses and Rainbows—named after the roses I gave mother on her last Valentine's day as a gesture of reconciliation, and the rainbow of all God's promises that He gave me after Mother's funeral.

Passing It On

Continuing across the platform, I heard my pastor talking about the seven women who had found their way to 509 Brandermill Road, and of how open and honest dialogue among trustworthy women had created a haven of hope. He described how we had built a safe, nonjudgmental place for one another, free of denominational boundaries, and how our focus had been on God and our friendships. My pastor wasn't intimidated by our work or threatened that we were reaching out into other churches and other denominations. "This group of women is not taking the place of what is going on in our churches," he said, "they are complementing the work of the church by making it real in their lives. They are taking biblical principles and sharing the different ways they have learned to apply them in practical ways in real-life situations."

And now it was my turn to speak. I scanned again the hundreds of faces before me, trying to look into each of their hurts. To anyone who needed it, I desperately wanted to pass along what

God had been showing me. I wanted each to see how God's Word is real and effective in our lives today. I wanted them to become Ephesians 3:20 believers. God's mighty power had taken my life's burdens and was transforming them into blessings, and I longed for each woman in that room to know that He stood ready to do it again and again and again!

I described my journey, sometimes with tears. And as the time came to conclude, I began to review my story with my audience.

"Who would believe a little girl wrought with devastation at such an innocent age, ripped from the arms of an unconditionally loving family and thrust into an abusive, addiction-driven environment, would survive?

"How could a four-year-old go from 'daddy's little princess' to being a mistake, as summed up in one overheard phrase: 'If only she had never been born'?

"How does she, at such a tender age, know instinctively how to conform to expectations, to appease and compromise in hopes of lightening the hand of her abuser? How does she hide the pain, stuff the agony, and yet sing in the choir as though nothing hurts? How does she make straight As, cheer at Friday night football games, and become Miss Teen Time, all the while indulging in such self-destructive tendencies as anorexia, diet pill addiction, depression, suicidal thoughts, and anxiety attacks?

"How does she become so adept at pretending? Where does she hang her mask when no one is looking?

"Where does she find the strength to battle day-to-day dysfunction when all she craves is the safety of a love she once knew? How does she manipulate life—her own and others'—so that all the deepest hurts in her heart remain secret? How does she manage to look so normal and engage in such a 'normal' life—school, dating, and eventually marriage and motherhood?

"How does she look those babies in the eyes and solemnly

vow that no matter what the cost, they will never know what she has known, they will never suffer the pain and the embarrassment? And how does she deliver on that promise when the cost is so personal, so invasive to all she has held most secret?

"How does she find the courage to tear down the walls of protectiveness she has built to shut out the possibility of pain? How does she open up her ugly brown paper bag—her heart—and let others see what lies within? How does she ask for help? How does she not only survive all this but somehow learn to thrive because of it?"

Standing before the women at the conference, I declared—and I declare to you today—that there is only one answer to all these questions. Ephesians 3:20 is the only explanation I have for my life.

Glory be to God,
who through His mighty power,
has taken my burdens and transformed them into blessings
and exceedingly abundantly more purpose and fulfillment
than I could have ever asked or even imagined!

MAKE IT YOURS

Celebrating Transformation

*D*ear friends, we've come a long way together and witnessed transparency and transformation in ourselves and others. One thing friends do together is to reminisce. Let's do that together now as a fitting way to honor our shared journey.

1. One person you met along this journey was the Samaritan woman. What transformation did you witness in her life?

2. I also introduced you to my mother. As you heard her story, what transformation did you notice?

3. You've heard a lot of my own story (perhaps too much of it!). How would you describe the transformation that God brought about in me?

4. Choices were required of all three of us for transformation to do its work. What choices did each of us make?

5. What choices might have brought about a different outcome?

6. I hope you worked through this book with other women. As you did, what transformations did you observe in them? List their names, and next to their names, place a word or phrase that sums up a change you saw take place as they participated in this study.

7. The beauty of walking through this book with other women is that we receive so many blessings from the others in our

groups. For each person in your group, complete the following sentence about how she has touched your life: "In sharing your burden with me, you blessed me by _____
_____."

8. And finally, how has pulling your burden from your bag begun a transformation in *your* life? You probably began this book convinced that your burdens had no purpose and were best left tucked away, out of sight. As you reached into your bag and faced your previously hidden hurts, regrets, abuse, and more, what happened within you? What have you done that you wouldn't have considered before? What steps have you taken that you never had the courage to take before? How are your perceptions changing—of yourself, of God, of others?

9. What would be your declaration today about how God can transform the burdens in your life?

Glory be to God,

who by His power working within me

has taken my burden of _____

and has already begun transforming it into blessings

exceedingly more than I could have ever imagined

by _____!

Journal Notes

ACKNOWLEDGMENTS

I would like to thank the many people who encouraged, supported, and helped me complete this book.

To my guys: Lee, Trey, and Austin, my prayers come true. Having you in my life gave me the desire and the courage to be the best I could for you. You know how I love you.

To Sue Kline, my friend, mentor, and editor: Your professional eye and years of experience helped me to clear the brush and let my passion shine through. And somehow, you made all the dreadful deadlines fun!

To the BroadStreet team: You have gone above and beyond to make my signature book one that truly reflects my heart and passion.

And to the hundreds of women (you know who you are) who have laughed with me, cried with me, and helped me refine my message: I am blessed to have you in my life!

ADDITIONAL RESOURCES

Books

Extend the Blessing: A Guided Journal

This guided journal walks you through one principle at a time from the *Burdens to Blessings* book. If you feel like you rushed through the book, then this is your invitation to slow down, sit with what you've read, let it put down roots in your heart and mind and bear fruit.

Burdens to Blessings: Young Adult Edition

Long before adulthood, girls learn to hide their hurt and shame. Bullying, peer pressure, abuse, loneliness, body image issues—these and similar pressures make it hard to face the future with hope. Kim Crabill brings her signature message of transformation and hope to young women from teens through twenties.

Infinitely More: Your 40-Day Ephesians 3:20 Adventure

Kim Crabill's life was transformed when she dared to believe God's promise in Ephesians 3:20—that He had the power to bring "infinitely more" to her life. Now she invites readers on a forty-day adventure of exploring what God has in store for *their* lives.

Cherished! 365 Readings That Celebrate God's Love for You

A compilation of bite-size readings from Kim's books and messages plus her *Daily Cup with Kim* e-mail devotionals. Spiral bound and formatted with room to journal.

Gift Booklets

These small booklets are designed for gift giving and fit easily into a standard-size envelope for mailing:

A Cup of Christmas: 31 Daily Readings for December

Are we ever more frazzled than at Christmas? This booklet brings back the wonder of the season. Its size lets you sip some encouragement in line at the mall or while stuck in traffic.

A Cup of Hope: 31 Daily Readings to Refresh You

When you've lost hope, you rarely get it back in one big swoop. More likely, you rediscover it through small steps and in daily doses. That's what this booklet offers: one page of hope each day, one verse, one prayer.

A Cup of Freedom: 31 Daily Readings to Send You Soaring

We have been set free, yet we so often live as if we were prisoners: of our thoughts, our pasts, the opinions of others, and more. These daily readings show the difference it makes when we embrace the freedom Christ offers us.

Video Teaching Series

Each series is available for digital download, is designed for group use, and includes:

- links to Kim Crabill's teaching videos to watch together;
- reproducible master copies of handouts (programs, teaching aids, etc.);
- discussion questions based on each video;
- suggested icebreakers for each session;
- FAQs about how to start and lead a small group;
- weekly teaching tips for the group leader;
- access to a ministry mentor to answer questions.

Burdens to Blessings

An eight-week video study to accompany Kim Crabill's signature book.

Perfectly Imperfect: Discover What a Perfect Fit You Are for God's Purposes

This eight-week video study visits eight imperfect women from the Bible who were a perfect fit for God's great purposes. An ideal follow-up to the *Burdens to Blessings* series.

The Power Within: Discover Your Surprising Power Source for Living

What if being Superwoman has nothing to do with a cape . . . and everything to do with a cross? This ten-week study explores the source of true, life-transforming power as revealed in the Beatitudes.

Spa for the Soul: 9 Treatments to Refresh Your Spirit

While most spa treatments focus on our exteriors, this nine-week video study introduces women to the treatments that refresh our weary souls.

All items can be ordered at RosesAndRainbows.org

ABOUT THE AUTHOR

Kim Crabill is the founder and president of Roses and Rainbows Ministries, Inc., and Community COFFEEs (Conversations of Friends of Faith to Encourage and Equip). Her message and passion come from her personal experience of longing to be used by God yet feeling unusable because of past abuse leading to anorexia, diet pill addiction, and depression. Her mother's deathbed challenge set Kim on a new path.

Kim has traveled nationally for more than twenty years, speaking at retreats, conferences, and to Bible study groups, and has been interviewed on national TV and radio. Kim draws upon personal experiences, biblical principles, and her training in counseling to inspire and challenge women to dare to be all God created them to be.

When not following her ministry passion, Kim follows her first passion of being a wife and mom. Kim and her husband, Lee, have been married thirty years and have two adult sons (and two shih tzus).

For more information about Kim, Roses and Rainbows Ministries, Inc., the nationwide Community COFFEE gatherings, and Kim's books and speaking engagements, visit

RosesAndRainbows.org